City Breaks in Dublin

REG BUTLER

In Association with

THOMSON HOLIDAYS

SETTLE PRESS

Text © 1996 Reg Butler

First published by Settle Press
10 Boyne Terrace Mews
London W11 3LR

ISBN (Paperback) 1 872876 47 1

Printed by Villiers Publications
19 Sylvan Avenue
London N3 2LE

Foreword

As Britain's leading short breaks specialist, we recognise the need for detailed information and guidance for CityBreak travellers. But much more is required than just a listing of museums and their opening times. For a few days, the CityBreak visitor wants to experience the local lifestyle.

We are therefore very pleased to work with Reg Butler and Settle Press on this latest addition to the CityBreak series of pocket guide-books.

For this book Reg Butler has collaborated closely with resident Dubliners who have year-round experience of helping visitors enjoy their city. We're sure you'll find this book invaluable in planning how to make best personal use of your time.

As well as CityBreaks in Dublin, other books in the series cover all the major capitals and art cities of Europe. Thomson also operate to many other world cities from departure points across the UK.

THOMSON CITYBREAKS

Contents

Chapter One

Alive, alive-oh in Dublin

If you need a good excuse for a few pints of Guinness, pop across to Dublin for a weekend dedicated to literature, music and architecture.

Dublin was European City of Culture in 1991. Even if you're a bit shaky on the works of James Joyce, Brendan Behan, Oscar Wilde and Samuel Beckett, you can follow in their footsteps for an evening's crash course that can help quench your thirst for literature and the spirit of Ireland.

A highly popular Dublin Literary Pub Crawl starts at 7.30 every night during summer, or at weekends only during winter. Professional actors lead you around the best-known literary pubs, with tongue-in-cheek stories at each location.

Brief scenes are performed, chosen for their humour. You get double value: an introduction or a refresher course to the great names of Irish literature, and a taster of their favourite pubs.

A similar educational programme is offered on the Musical Pub Crawl. Led by a professional musician, you can singalong in traditional Irish style, taking good care to stop your throat drying out. Some singing pubs revive the beautiful old melodies which Grandma knew and loved.

It's a pleasant way of spending an evening, wallowing in Guinness and nostalgia.

For dedicated students of music, Dublin can also claim to be the world's Rock Music Capital, thanks to the local talent of U2, The Hothouse Flowers, Thin Lizzy, Moving Hearts and singers like Bob Geldof and Chris de Burgh.

Rock 'n Stroll

Much of this hothouse talent flowered in the warm and friendly pub atmosphere, just like The Chieftains and The Dubliners in the 1960s.

The helpful Dublin Tourism office has organised a Rock 'n Stroll Trail that zig-zags across the city centre. Drop in and listen at any of the music pubs, and maybe you can boast in a few years' time that you first heard the latest hit band during your Dublin weekend in the 1990s.

Some of these pubs are wildly popular, jam-packed every night. Just try to squeeze into O'Donoghues in Merrion Row, where The Dubliners made their name during the folk revival of the sixties. It's still a centre for traditional music.

Sometimes the musical and literary trails overlap. In his autobiography, Bob Geldof relates how his Boomtown Rats used to meet in a famous cafe called Bewley's in Grafton Street.

Bewley's has been a great meeting place for tea, coffee and talk for many decades. Open almost round the clock, it offers a hearty breakfast all day – bacon, egg, sausage, tomato, hash browns, black and white pudding, two slices of toast, a pot of tea or a mug of cofffee for £3.60.

On the first floor is the James Joyce Room where so many literary folk have gossipped.

Another floor higher is Bewley's Museum Restaurant, which recreates the charm of a Victorian teashop. Here is starting point for a lively Dublin Footsteps tour that covers Literary and Georgian Dublin.

During the 18th century fashionable Dublin was laid out with superbly designed streets and squares and public buildings. On the River Liffey waterfront, the Custom House is one of the finest buildings in Dublin.

Leinster House was the grandest of stately mansions, now used by the Irish parliament. Facing Leinster House is Merrion Square, the world's best-preserved stretch of Georgian architecture.

Giants of literature

Here Oscar Wilde spent his boyhood. Numerous wall plaques around Merrion Square commemorate other literary and political giants such as Sheridan the playright, W.B. Yeats who won the Nobel Prize for Poetry, and Daniel O'Connell the 19th-century politician.

The nationalist leader is honoured with a major monument in O'Connell Street, where the Easter Rising of 1916 erupted. The Irish view of that trauma is displayed in the National Museum, beside Leinster House. A gallery called Road to Independence covers the years 1900-1923.

Most of the key sightseeing of Dublin is central and within easy walking range. Next bridge along from O'Connell is the pedestrian Ha'penny Bridge which leads direct into the Temple Bar area. This former derelict zone has been restored to trendy new life. Cobbled streets are lined with craft shops, galleries and art exhibitions, while pubs, cafes and restaurants stay lively until late.

Dublin cuisine has now gone international, with fullest ethnic choice from across Europe and Asia. Irish stew is harder to find on local menus. You won't hear Molly Malone crying "Cockles and mussels alive, alive-oh!" but Dublin still has a good reputation for seafood dishes.

Molly Malone's memory lives on, with the song that's almost like the Dublin National Anthem. Most of her "streets broad and narrow" are still in place. Some bar and shop signs are painted in the curly script that would make Queen Victoria feel it was still her century.

A talkative Irishman will quite likely inform you that "Last year the Irish summer fell on a Sunday." But there are compensations, like no currency problems. Everywhere you get friendly service, in hotels, bars, restaurants and on the buses. It's a joy to listen to the honey-voiced charm of the Irish. And no Continental country can compete with the traditional Irish breakfast of bacon, eggs and properly-made tea!

Chapter Two
Arrival in Dublin

2.1 Choice of routes

Aer Lingus operates direct flights to Dublin from Birmingham, Bristol, East Midlands, Edinburgh, Glasgow, Leeds/Bradford, London Heathrow, Manchester and Newcastle. Direct transatlantic services are operated from New York, Boston and Chicago.

Ryanair flies to Dublin from Prestwick, Manchester, Liverpool, Birmingham, Stansted, Luton and Gatwick.

Other services operate from Blackpool, Bournemouth, Cardiff, Exeter, Humberside, London City Airport and Newquay.

Ferries sail from Holyhead to Dublin by Irish Ferries in 3 hours 30 minutes, with local bus 53 to the centre.

Stena Line has introduced a 50-mph High Speed Superferry which does Holyhead to Dun Laoghaire in 1 hour 40 minutes. Frequent DART (Dublin Area Rapid Transit) trains connect with Dublin centre.

Airport buses
Bus 41 takes about 40 minutes from the Airport to Dublin's Central Bus Station, costing only £1.10. But most people prefer the express Airlink service costing £2.50, for a 17-minute journey. Airlink operates three or four services every hour and is equipped for carrying luggage – which is not so with Bus 41.

Into the centre

The journey goes a short distance along the M1 Motorway, which then becomes a regular road through the northern suburbs of Dublin. The distance from airport to centre is 12 kilometres. Ireland has gone completely metric on the highways. Street signs and road names are bilingual – Gaelic on the top line, English below.

The Central Bus Station, which the locals call Bus Áras, is located on the north bank of the River Liffey, close to the Custom House. *See the orientation map on pages 14/15, fig. 12.*

It has a currency exchange kiosk which charges less commission than the Bank of Ireland at the airport. There are baggage store facilities, and you can start to inform yourself on Dublin's bus system.

Taxis

Outside the Bus Station is a cab rank. Meters start at £1.80, with 40p extra for luggage. Distances to central hotels are small, and the total cost will be around £3. A 10% tip is normal. From the airport to your central hotel would cost between £12 and £15 by taxi. Taxis ordered by phone charge £1.20 extra.

2.2 Orientation

Dublin lies about midway down the east coast of Ireland. The River Liffey flows east through the city, dividing it into two halves, north and south. The eastern boundaries of the city lie along Dublin Bay and the Irish Sea.

On the southern and south-western fringes of the city are the Wicklow and Dublin Mountains. To the north and northwest of Dublin city and county are the flat plains of Kildare and Meath.

The central area north of the Liffey is focussed on O'Connell Street (*see map, fig. 1*), with the main sightseeing highlights on that side of the river all within a few minutes' walk.

11

South Dublin

Just south of O'Connell Bridge is Trinity College (*see map, fig. 16*), the Bank of Ireland and Grafton Street (*fig. 23*), with easy walking to all the central sites. The southern boundary of sightseeing interest is the Grand Canal, originally built to link the River Shannon with the capital.

City buses

A network of 130 bus routes operates within the city, using double-deckers, single decks and mini-buses. But in Dublin's compact centre there is really little need of public transport. Short hops by bus cost 55p, and that's enough for most journeys. A one-day adult bus pass costs £3.30.

Information Centre

The Dublin Tourism Centre is now located in the de-sanctified St Andrews Presbyterian church at the end of Suffolk Street, right opposite O'Neills pub (*see map, fig. 17*). This very central location, close to the Bank of Ireland and Grafton Street, occupies a historic site from Viking times.

The interior of the former church has been totally remodelled, with information counters on the ground floor, a giftware shop, a coffee shop upstairs, and a computerised touch-vision system for information about attractions.

A number of signposted city walking tours start from this location. Several trails have been marked out: Georgian Heritage; Old City Heritage; and Cultural Heritage.

2.3 Sightseeing strategy

Probably 90% of Dublin's attractions are within easy walking distance of O'Connell Bridge. The rest can be reached by a short bus-ride. This guide-book focusses on six recommended circuits which could each take around three hours, depending on your depth of interest.

1 – **O'Connell Street**: O'Connell Bridge; Statue; GPO; Parnell column
2 – **Moore Street Market**
3 – **Gate Theatre**
4 – **Parnell Square**: Garden of Remembrance; Findlaters Church; Writers Museum; Hugh Lane Gallery
5 – **Wax Museum**
6 – **James Joyce Centre**
7 – **Belvedere College**
8 – **Mountjoy Square**
9 – **St Mary's Pro-Cathedral**: Tyrone House
10 – **Abbey Theatre**
11 – **Liberty Hall**
12 – **Custom House**: Bus Station; Custom House Dock
13 – **Four Courts**
14 – **Irish Whiskey Centre**
15 – **Direction**: to Collins Barracks (for National Museum); Phoenix Park
16 – **College Green**: Trinity College; Bank of Ireland & Art Centre
17 – **Dublin Tourism Centre**
18 – **Temple Bar & Halfpenny Bridge**
19 – **Dublin Castle**: City Hall
20 – **Christchurch Cathedral**: Dublinia
21 – **St Patrick's Cathedral**: Marsh's Library
22 – **Guinness Hop Store**: direction to Phoenix Park; Kilmainham Hospital & the Gaol
23 – **Grafton Street area**: Powerscourt Shopping Centre; Civic Museum
24 – **Leinster House**: Parliament; National Gallery; National Museums; Gov't Bldgs.
25 – **Merrion Square**
26 – **Fitzwilliam Street**: Number Twenty Nine
27 – **Fitzwilliam Square**
28 – **St Stephen's Green**
29 – **Newman House**
30 – **Mansion House**
31 - **Bernard Shaw House Museum**

CENTRAL DUBLIN

⌗ River & Canals

╋▬■▬╋ DART Rail Station

0 metres 500

North Street

Eccles St

Mountjoy St

Dorset Street

Temple St

Denmark St

King's Inns

Dominick Street

Parnell Square

5

4

3

O'Connell

Moore St

2

Capel Street

Parnell

North King Street

Blackhall Pl.

Queen St

Smithfield

Bow St

Church Street

St Mary's Lane

Mary St

Henry St

1

14

Chancery St

Abbey Street

Bachelors

15

Ellis Qy

Arran Quay

Inns Qy

Ormond Quay

Wellington Quay

Aston

Usher's Quay

Merchants Quay

13

18

20 †

Lord Edward St

Dame Street

17

22

Thomas St

High St

Francis St

Werburgh St

19

Georges St

Wicklow S

Meath St

Patrick St

Stephen St

William St

23

Pimblico

The Coombe

Bride St

Aungier St

King St

Ardee St

21 †

Kevin St

York St

Cork Street

New St

Kevin St

Cuffe St

29

Donore Ave

Mangan Road

Long Lane

Heytesbury St

Camden St

Harcourt Street

Dufferin Ave

Clanbrassil St

Synge St

Richmond St

Ha

Ade

31

South Circular Road

Charlemo

Grand Canal

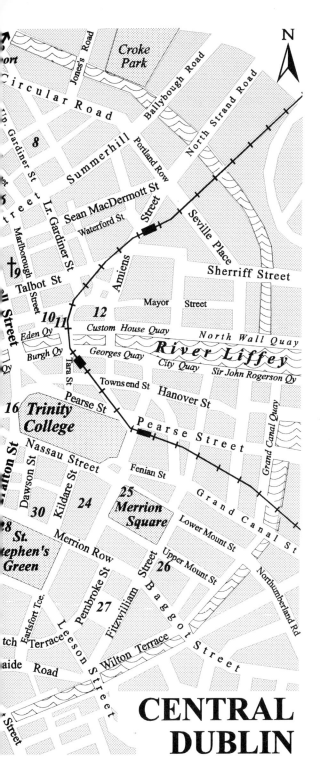

CENTRAL
DUBLIN

Which chapter?

Chapter 3 looks at the area around O'Connell Street, and sites north of the Liffey.

Chapter 4 concentrates on Trinity College, the Bank of Ireland and the trendy urban renewal area of Temple Bar (*see map, fig. 18*).

Chapter 5 considers the main shopping area of pedestrianized Grafton Street and the surrounding district, with a break for fresh air in St Stephen's Green (*fig. 28*). This area is also thick with pubs and bars that have literary or music associations.

Chapter 6 takes a stroll through the best of Dublin's Georgian squares, many linked with the great names of Irish literature and politics.

Chapter 7 covers the medieval area of Dublin, first settled by early Christians, then Vikings and finally the Normans. That covers the Cathedral located where St Patrick preached in the 5th century, Dublin Castle which was founded by the Vikings, and Christ Church Cathedral rebuilt by the Anglo-Normans. *See map, figs. 19, 20 & 21.*

Chapter 8 goes to areas like Kilmainham and Phoenix Park, for which transport is needed. *See direction pointers on the map, figs. 15 & 22.*

Special interest museums

If your main interest is in **Literary Dublin**, then it's worth starting at the Dublin Writers Museum in Parnell Square, with a James Joyce Centre very close. *See map, figs. 4 & 6.*

The Shaw birthplace at 33 Synge Street is a 15-minute walk from St Stephen's Green, or can be reached by buses 16, 19 or 22. *Map, fig. 31.*

For **Political Dublin**, the National Museum (*see map, fig. 24*) displays the Irish viewpoint in a gallery called The Road to Independence. The Wax Museum (*see map, fig. 5*) around the corner from Parnell Square displays historical figures in period settings, with a recorded commentary on the principal events. To complete the picture, visit Kilmainham Gaol, reached by buses number 23, 51, 51A, 78 or 79.

For **Art-gallery Dublin**, the essentials are the Hugh Lane Gallery in Parnell Square (*see map, fig. 4*) and the National Gallery of Ireland in Merrion Square (*fig. 25*).

For **Early and Medieval Dublin**, the National Museum has a superb collection of prehistoric Ireland from the Stone and Bronze Ages, gold treasures, and Viking Age Ireland. Dublinia – adjoining Christ Church Cathedral – gives an audio-visual presentation of medieval life from the arrival of the Anglo-Normans in 1170, until the closure of the monasteries in 1540.

The five key museums are described in Chapter 9; Dublinia in Chapter 7.

If you visit Dublin during autumn, winter or early springtime, take careful note of opening times. Some attractions operate restricted hours during the low season, like 11-16 hrs; while others still keep to the routine of 10-17 hrs or 17.30. Plan your day to avoid disappointment.

2.4 Guided tours

For an overall view of Dublin, it's worth taking a general sightseeing tour before concentrating on the areas in which you have the deepest interest.

The Dublin Bus company offers several choices, all starting from 59 Upper O'Connell Street. A **Panoramic Tour** features the main central highlights, both sides of River Liffey and out to Kilmainham and Phoenix Park. The tour lasts 2¾ hours, costs £8, and operates daily year-round at 10.15 and 14.15 hrs.

Owing to the reputation of Ireland's weather, these tours are not operated with open-top buses. But it's certainly worth getting onto the top deck of the double-decker, for an upwardly mobile view of the city. The driver does the commentary in a rich Irish voice which is a pleasure in itself.

The central area alone is covered by the **Heritage Tour** with departures every half hour on a circuit with eight special bus stops en route. An all-day ticket costing £5 enables you to hop on and off as often as you wish.

Similar Dublin City tours are operated with open-top double-deckers – better for photography – by **Gray Line** and by **Guide Friday**. They each charge £6 with the same hop-on, hop-off system through the day. Their itineraries are slightly wider than those followed by the Heritage Tour above.

A **South Coast** tour costing £9, departing daily at 11 a.m., follows the coast past Bray and Greystones, and returns by an inland mountain route.

Walking tours
Catering for different interests, there is choice of several daytime or evening walking tours in Dublin centre.

By day, walking tours called Dublin Footsteps begin from Bewley's Museum Restaurant in Grafton Street (*see map, fig. 23*). Typical circuits are a Literary Walk starting at 11 hrs, or a Medieval Walk at 14.30 hrs. Another variant is a combined Literary and Georgian Walk.

Historical Walking Tours are organised by history graduates of Trinity College, starting from the main gate of the College. These operate daily at 11, 12 and 15 hrs.

For James Joyce devotees, a walking tour of Joyce's Dublin is possible, by advance arrangement only. It starts from the James Joyce Centre at 25 North Great George's Street. *See map, fig. 6*. Tel: 873 1984.

Chapter Three
North of the Liffey

3.1 O'Connell Street

Until the late 17th century, the north side of the River Liffey was undeveloped. Then came a dramatic change, when the 1st Duke of Ormonde, the viceroy of Ireland, had a great vision to transform Dublin from just another medieval town into a real capital city.

Land was reclaimed eastwards towards the sea, river banks were controlled by walls and a wide road was built along the north bank. A second bridge was built in 1678. The decision was then made to develop in style on the north side.

Here was the start of Georgian Dublin. 'Georgian' is used loosely to describe the 18th century, covered by the reigns of four consecutive King Georges from 1714 to 1830. This is when Georgian squares and architecture were created.

The first developments in early 18th century were at the top end of present-day O'Connell Street. The squares behind it now look rather shabby, but initially they were very grand.

O'Connell Street was a quiet residential cul-de-sac called Drogheda Street which ended short of the river. Drogheda Street was named after the developer, Henry Moore, Earl of Drogheda, who named other streets after himself: Henry Street, Moore Street, Earl Street and Off Street.

Those four street names still survive, but Drogheda was later changed to Sackville, and then to O'Connell Street in 1890. *Map, fig. 1.*

Highway planning

Meanwhile, a later developer bought the estate in 1749, and greatly widened the central street to its present building line. This followed a policy of the Wide Street Commission which held a powerful city planning function. In contrast to the haphazard narrow medieval layout of central Dublin on the south side, wide streets were regarded as the hallmark of a true capital city.

With the ongoing development north of the river, the city was building more bridges. Previously there had been just one crossing at Dublin, across a bridge established in 1214.

In 1794, the Carlisle Bridge was opened, renamed in 1890 as O'Connell Bridge. It directly linked the grand residential developments north of the river, to Parliament House (today's Bank of Ireland) and Trinity College. *Map, fig. 16.*

The bridge, rebuilt in 1880, converted the former residential cul-de-sac into the main north-south thoroughfare that runs through the city centre. Unusually for a bridge, it's about as broad as it's long.

Since the building of the bridge, O'Connell Street has become the most famous thoroughfare in Dublin, playing a leading role in the city's commercial and political history.

The street and the bridge are named after Daniel O'Connell, whose monument faces the bridge. Thanks to his untiring eloquence, the Catholic Emancipation Act was passed by the British Parliament in 1829. This reversed the penal laws of the 1690s, which had aimed at discouraging the practice of Roman Catholicism. Historically, O'Connell is known as The Liberator.

The figures beneath his statue represent the arts, trades and professions of Ireland. What look like angels just up from a coal-mine, are the winged virtues of Courage, Eloquence, Fidelity and Patriotism. One angel is marked by gunfire from the fighting that raged along O'Connell Street during the Easter Rising of 1916.

Post Office that made history

The General Post Office is the white building with an Ionic portico. Opened in 1818, it was designed by Francis Johnston who had also been responsible for a neighbouring monument to Nelson. On Easter Monday 1916, this GPO building was seized by Irish rebels and was used as the headquarters of their uprising.

A commemorative plaque inside one of the GPO entrances says: "Here, on Easter Monday 1916, Patrick Pearse read the proclamation of the Irish Republic from this building. And from this building he commanded the forces that asserted in arms Ireland's right to freedom."

In the fighting that followed, the GPO and most other buildings in O'Connell Street were almost totally destroyed by shellfire. The GPO was rebuilt during the 1920s, precisely as Francis Johnston had designed it.

Other buildings along O'Connell Street were reconstructed during the 1920s and 1930s. The former architectural grandeur has disappeared, but the street still keeps some of its original handsome style. Especially attractive is the great width of the street, with a number of monuments spaced among the trees down the centre.

Facing the GPO is Clery's department store, established last century. Under Clery's Clock has long been a traditional meeting place and is where many a Dublin romance has begun.

Across from Clery's is a statue of a labour leader of the Irish Transport and General Workers Union who made a rousing speech here during a General Strike and lock-out of 1913. With his arms raised aloft, Big Jim Larkin seems to be asking "Will it ever stop raining?"

A Nelson's Pillar, erected in 1809, was just as much a city landmark as Nelson's Column in London. But the monument was blown up in 1966, to mark the 50th anniversary of the Easter Rising. Nelson's head is now housed in the Dublin Civic Museum in South William Street.

The millenium jacuzzi

Further along is the Anna Livia commemorative fountain, installed in 1988 to celebrate Dublin's official millenium. Anna Livia is the mythical spirit of the River Liffey, but has acquired all kinds of other descriptions: 'the belle in the swell'; 'the bride in the tide'; 'the flower in the shower'. But her designer, Jim Fitzpatrick, called her 'the floosie in the jacuzzi.'

The tall column at the northern end of O'Connell Street is dedicated to Charles Stuart Parnell. He led the Irish party in the British Parliament from 1875 until 1890. On the verge of achieving Home Rule for Ireland, Parnell's campaign collapsed through his exposure in a divorce scandal with Kitty O'Shea, the wife of another politician.

Among the other monuments along O'Connell Street is a statue of a famed revolutionary, William Smith O'Brien. He led the Young Ireland movement and rebellion in 1848. He was transported to Tasmania, but escaped and went to the United States. He died during the American Civil War as a colonel in the Union Army.

Sir John Gay (1816-75) on a horse is a man who never smiled, despite his cheerful name. He organised Dublin's water supply from County Wicklow in the 1860s.

Moore Street market

Halfway along O'Connell Street, close to the GPO, is the pedestrianised Henry Street with Arnott's department store and numerous street vendors.

The first turning right off Henry Street is the Moore Street fruit, flower and vegetable market. A mosaic design made in 1993 marks the entrance. Moore Street echoes to the sound of stallholders' crying their wares, and selling out-dated chocolate bars cheap. *See map, fig. 2.*

The vendors are famed for their speed of repartee, rather like the traditional Cockney barrow boys of London. But you probably won't hear anything more witty than a barrow lady chanting "ten bananas a pound". It's a good location for colourful photos, and you may even catch the rare sight of a sturdy cart-horse, bringing in produce. The ILAC shopping centre along one side of Moore Street is crammed with discount trash.

Moore Street leads into Parnell Street. This was formerly Great Britain Street, renamed in 1928. The Rotunda across the street can claim around 240 years of hard labour. The Rotunda Maternity Hospital opened its doors in 1757, and claims to be the oldest Protestant maternity hospital in the British Isles.

Alongside, the Rotunda Assembly Rooms were built in 1764 as an entertainment complex, which included a ballroom, a theatre, a gambling casino and a supper room. The profits were used to finance the Maternity Hospital. *See map, fig. 3.*

Since 1930, the **Gate Theatre** has occupied the former supper room. It rapidly built a strong dramatic tradition with an avant garde approach to Irish and European productions. Orson Welles and James Mason began their careers here.

3.2 Parnell Square

Originally called Rutland Square, here was the first of Dublin's magnificent Georgian housing developments, laid out during the 1750s and completed by 1767. *See map, fig. 4.*

During the late 18th century, virtually every house was inhabited by a duke or an earl or an MP. But then, after the Act of Union of 1801, many of them moved to London.

Possibly the finest mansion in Dublin was built for Lord Charlemont, a great arts patron who doubled as Commander-in-Chief of the Irish Volunteers, an army of 100,000 men. The building came into public ownership in 1863, and now houses the **Hugh Lane Municipal Gallery of Modern Art**, which is exceptionally rich in the Impressionists.

European Cultural Capital

A close neighbour is the **Dublin Writers Museum** at 18 and 19 Parnell Square. The city has produced a disproportionate number of writers of international repute. The museum was opened in 1991 to mark Dublin's year as the Cultural Capital of Europe. *(See chapter 9 for Museum details, and also for the Hugh Lane Gallery).*

On the corner of the square is the **Abbey Presbyterian Church** dating from the 1860s. It is better known among Dubliners as Findlater's Church. Alexander Findlater was a Scotsman who came to Dublin in the 1830s, made his fortune as a retail wine merchant and grocer, and paid for the church construction.

On Parnell Square East is the entrance to the **Garden of Remembrance**. It opened in 1966 on the 50th anniversary of the Easter Rising, and is dedicated to the memory of all who died in the cause of Irish independence. Mosaics depict weapons made redundant by the peace process. A sculpture by Oisín Kelly is based on the legend of children who were turned into swans.

Opposite, at 5 Parnell Square East is the birthplace of a distinguished surgeon, wit and author, Oliver St. John Gogarty. But he is more famous as the model for Buck Mulligan, the opening character in James Joyce's novel *Ulysses*. He never forgave Joyce for making him better known as Buck Mulligan than ever he achieved as an author in his own right.

Virtually every corner of central Dublin can claim associations with the James Joyce novel, which depicts just one day – Bloomsday, 16 June 1904 – when Leopold Bloom wandered on his Odyssey through the city.

In a parallel street to Parnell Square East is the **James Joyce Centre** in a beautifully restored Georgian house at 35 North Great George's Street. *See map, fig. 6.* The Centre aims to promote an interest in the author's life and works. For those who are less than devoted to James

Joyce, the house itself is worth visiting for its superb plasterwork by the 18th century master craftsman Michael Stapleton.

Open Tue-Sat 10.00-16.30; Sun 12.30-16.30 hrs. Entrance £2 for the house only; £5 for the house plus a one-hour guided walk through the Joyce territory of north Dublin. Tel: 878 8547.

Very close is Belvedere College (*see map, fig. 7*) where Jame Joyce went to secondary school. He describes his schooldays there in *A Portrait of the Artist as a Young Man*.

A few blocks further out is **Mountjoy Square**, another great Georgian residential area, built between 1792 and 1818. *See map, fig. 8.* The district later became very shabby. Many houses declined into the slum tenements that Sean O'Casey wrote about in the 20th century. The playwright lived at no. 35, and used 'Hilljoy Square' as the setting for *The Shadow of a Gunman*. Efforts are being made to restore the area.

3.3 East of O'Connell Street

Return to O'Connell Street, and take first left into Catha Brugha Street. This very short turning was laid out only in the 1920s when O'Connell Street was under reconstruction. It leads into Sean MacDermott Street, which formerly was Gloucester Street.

Here's another James Joyce *Ulysses* connection: the area of Dublin that he terms Nighttown. At the turn of the century the district was known as Monto, a notorious red light zone. It was all cleaned up in the 1920s.

On Marlborough Street is **St Mary's Catholic Pro-cathedral**, built in the 1820s, the principal Catholic church of Dublin. *See map, fig. 9.* (Both cathedrals south of the Liffey are Protestant). Opposite is a fine Georgian mansion, built 1742 and named **Tyrone House** after its original owner, Viscount Tyrone. It is now occupied by offices of the Department of Education.

Abbey Theatre

Along Lower Abbey Street stands the uninspiring building of the Abbey Theatre (*see map, fig. 10*), giving no hint of the creative sparkle within. It was designed by Michael Scott, who also built the central Bus Station. The present structure replaces the theatre which caught fire in 1951.

Ever since 1904, the Irish National Theatre Society has supported Irish playwrights, and The Abbey has maintained a world reputation as Ireland's leading theatre. Especially it became famous through controversial plays by John Millington Synge and Sean O'Casey. Two of their respective works – *The Playboy of the Western World* and *The Plough and the Stars* – caused first-night riots when shown in 1907 and 1926.

Certainly most theatre-lovers on a Dublin visit will want to attend a performance in the Abbey, which is so rich in theatrical legend. A second auditorium called The Peacock is located in the basement, and gives experimental productions.

Opposite the theatre, The Plough pub is frequented by theatre devotees. The Flowing Tide also has great character. Theatre posters decorate not only the walls, but also the entire ceilings.

Further along Abbey Street is the Irish Life Centre, opened in the early 1980s. On the forecourt is an exciting piece of modern sculpture entitled *Reason triumphant over the emotions*. It was created by Oisín Kelly who specialised in outdoor sculpture during his short lifetime.

The tall glass building is **Liberty Hall**, the loftiest building in Dublin, vintage 1960s. *See map, fig. 11*. At 197 feet high, it even has what looks like a wavy umbrella on top to keep the roof dry. Liberty Hall houses the Services, Industrial, Professional and Technical Union which originated in 1908 as the Irish Transport and General Workers' Union. Today, no building of that height would get planning permission. Since the 1970s, the height of any new building is restricted to 80 feet or six storeys.

3.4 Custom House

Virtually next door to Liberty Hall is the superb Custom House (*see map, fig. 12*), which rates as the finest building in Dublin. It was designed by a London architect named James Gandon.

When he was asked in 1779 to design and supervise the building of a new Custom House on reclaimed land, he was reluctant to accept the commission. Gandon's main reason was that he had heard all kinds of rumours concerning the sobriety or otherwise of Irish workmen.

When Gandon arrived, he insisted on bringing with him some 300 English artisans and labourers. After only three weeks in Dublin, he came to the conclusion that the English workers were even less sober than their Irish counterparts. He fired the lot, and hired Irishmen in their places.

The Custom House took ten years to build, and opened in 1791. Gandon was always fond of placing large stone figures above the entrances to his buildings. The figure topping the dome is the lady Commerce looking out to sea. That sculpture was carved by Edward Smyth, a Dublin man who worked exclusively with Gandon.

The four standing figures above the front entrance are (left to right) Mercury, Industry, Plenty and Neptune. Currently the building houses two government departments – Environment and Health. Another splendid view of the Custom House and its gracious outline is from Georges Quay on the south bank of the River Liffey.

After completion of the Custom House, Gandon remained in Dublin for the rest of his life, designing many magnificent buildings for Dublin and around Ireland.

The Custom House Docks – east of the Custom House – were initially another 18th-century development on reclaimed land. The dockyard has now been redeveloped as an international financial services centre.

3.5 Four Courts

On the north bank of the River Liffey, upstream from Halfpenny Bridge, is Ormond Quay, dating from the late 17th century and lined with former merchant houses. Ships tied up here, well into the 18th century.

For anyone making the James Joyce pilgrimage, the Ormond Hotel is where all the main characters of *Ulysses* converge in the middle of Bloomsday afternoon. A plaque recalls this historic event. Fans of Joyce come here for special celebrations every year on Bloomsday, June 16.

Past O'Donovan Rossa Bridge on Inns Quay is the **Four Courts** group of law courts, another classical masterpiece designed by James Gandon and completed in 1802. *See map, fig. 13.* Several centuries of public records were destroyed in the opening phase of Ireland's civil war in 1922, when Free State forces attacked anti-Treaty forces with field-guns. Rebuilding took nine years, to restore the complex to its original state, except for the dome which is not a faithful replica.

The next bridge along, called Father Matthew Bridge, is located on the site of the original medieval crossing, where the Normans built the first bridge across the Liffey in 1214. Father Theobald Matthew (1790-1856) was the Apostle of Temperance who is also honoured with a statue in O'Connell Street.

Irish Whiskey Corner

Despite Father Matthew, a detour from the quayside is worth considering, to visit the Irish Whiskey Corner on Bow Street, at the site of the old Jameson Whiskey Distillery. Tours include a 15-minute documentary film, visit to a museum and tasting in a 1920's style bar. *See map, fig. 14.*

Tour times in May-Oct are Mon-Fri at 11, 14.30 and 15.30 hrs; Sat at 14.30 and 15.30 only. Sun at 15.30 only. Nov-Apr Mon-Fri at 15.30 only. Phone 872 5566 to check timings.

3.6 Collins Barracks

Further along towards Phoenix Park, on Wolfe Tone Quay, is the former Collins Barracks, which is under conversion for use by the National Museum. *For direction, see map, fig. 15.*

It was used as a barracks from 1703 until July 1994. Until then, it was the world's oldest purpose-built military barracks in continuous occupation as such.

From the 1850s until 1922, it was known as the Royal Barracks – home to the Royal Dublin Fusiliers. That was a regular army regiment, seeing action in many campaigns in which the British army was involved.

There were appalling losses in 1915 when men of the Royal Dublin Fusiliers landed at Suvla Bay during the Gallipoli campaign. Very few survived. Most of the men of that regiment were drawn from the mean tenements of the Dublin slums. Virtually every family was affected by those great losses.

In the future, Collins Barracks will become the National Museum, while the present building in Findlay Street will be converted to other uses. The first stage of the museum project will open in late 1996 or early 1997. The emphasis of the new displays will be on the history, arts, crafts and traditions of Ireland since the 17th century.

Chapter Four

Around College Green

4.1 Trinity College

Trinity College Dublin – TCD for short – is the sole constituent college of Dublin University, founded by royal charter of Queen Elizabeth 1 in 1592, and established on the site of a confiscated monastery. In social and academic prestige, Trinity ranks almost equal to Oxbridge. *Map, fig. 16.*

During the past four centuries, most of the great names of Irish history, politics, religion and literature have studied here, including Jonathan Swift, Oscar Wilde and Samuel Beckett.

At the entrance are statues of two famous graduates, Oliver Goldsmith and Edmund Burke, the finest orator of the 18th century.

TCD houses a world renowned 'copyright library' which has been entitled since 1801 to receive a free copy of every book published in Britain and Ireland. Trinity's greatest treasure is a richly illuminated copy of the Gospels, the Book of Kells, dating from the 8th century and regarded as the world's most beautiful book.

Founded as a Protestant university to 'establish true religion within the realm', TCD did not admit Catholics until 1793. Religious restrictions were not finally lifted until 1873, but female students were admitted from 1903.

Trinity College occupies a superb 40-acre site in the heart of the city, giving it a unique central place in the social and political life of Dublin.

From Georgian to concrete modernism

The quadrangles are wide open to the public. Most of the university buildings are Georgian, with almost nothing earlier than 18th century. The most modern building, of 20th-century concrete, is the Arts and Social Sciences block, which includes the Douglas Hyde Gallery of Modern Art and a Samuel Beckett centre. Sculptures on the lawn are by Pomodoro, Alexander Calder and Henry Moore.

From late May through September an audiovisual display called *The Dublin Experience* tells the Dublin story over the past thousand years. Open daily 10-17 hrs. Entrance £3.

The Colonnades, with the Book of Kells and the Long Room library, comprise the most visited attraction in Dublin. To avoid the overcrowding of peak season, an individual sightseer should plan to visit during lunchtime – when the coach tour groups have finished their morning circuits, and before the afternoon trips begin. Open Mon-Sat 9.30-17.30 hrs; Sun (Jun-Sep) 9.30-17 hrs; Sun (Oct-May) 12-17 hrs. Entrance £3.50.

A visit starts in the Library Shop, passes through the Colonnades area which is now used for temporary exhibitions, and on to the Book of Kells and the Old Library; returning through the Library Shop.

Book of Kells

Dating from about 800 AD, the manuscript is a marriage of Irish calligraphy, art and decoration with the Latin text of the four Gospels. The book was probably the work of the monastic community of Iona, and was held at the church of Kells in County Meath, some 30 miles northwest of Dublin.

Certainly it remained at Kells from the year 1007 until 1654. It was then moved to Dublin for safety during the Cromwellian period, and was presented to Trinity College in 1661.

Decorating the Gospels

The 680-page book was created by four scribes, backed by a number of artists who worked on the production over several years. Individual parchment leaves are made from calf skin, otherwise known as vellum. Kept in a climatically-controlled display case, the Book of Kells is opened at a different page about once a month.

The decoration of each Gospel is so rich and brilliant that an entire page is taken up with ornamentation of just the first word alone. It is virtually impossible for a layman to identify where that first word exists amid all the intricate detail.

To study the work at leisure, a facsimile edition has been published in a limited edition of 1400 copies. If you need it for your home bookshelves, the price per copy is US $ 18,000.

Two other early medieval manuscripts are also on display: the Book of Mulling; and the earlier Book of Durrow, which dates from about 675 AD. Both of them contain the four Gospels in Latin, with ornamentation.

The Long Room

Trinity College Library ranks among the world's great research institutions, with around three million volumes spread among eight buildings. The oldest of these buildings is the Long Room, over 200 feet in length, established between 1712 and 1732 to house the growing collections of books and manuscripts.

Originally this Georgian library was a one-storeyed room with a plaster ceiling. During the last century the ceiling deteriorated, so it was rebuilt into a two-storied structure with a barrel-vaulted roof. This superbly beautiful library room, holding 200,000 books, has arranged a 3-year exhibition on the Book of Kells and its background, to run until 1999.

Also on show is one of the few copies of the 1916 Independence Proclamation that remain from the original printing of 2,500 leaflets.

After a visit, you can walk through the grounds to the playing fields at the back. A pedestrian exit – the Lincoln Place gate – comes out near the corner by Merrion Square.

Otherwise, exit onto Nassau Street, or onto College Green to face the Bank of Ireland.

4.2 Bank of Ireland

Opposite the main entrance of Trinity College is Dublin's most noticeable monument, with stately Ionic and Corinthian porticos. It's the 18th-century Parliament House which has been occupied by the Bank of Ireland since 1803. *Map, fig. 16.*

Designed by Edward Lovatt Pearce, the stately building was completed in 1739, but enlarged later. An Irish Parliament had been established in 1661 with two Houses, for Lords and Commons.

This Parliament was open to Protestants only. Less than 5% of the population had any voice in how membership should be composed. All decisions then had to be ratified by the Parliament in Westminster.

This continued until the Act of Union of 1801 which united the Irish and the British Parliaments in London. The redundant Irish Parliament building was sold two years later for £40,000 to the Bank of Ireland, a fast-expanding commercial bank with a client list mainly of aristocrats and wealthy merchants.

The House of Commons was converted into the present Cash Office, and the House of Lords became the board room. Apart from when a board meeting is held, the House of Lords can be freely visited during banking hours – 10-15 hrs Mon-Fri and until 17 hrs on Thursdays. Informal armchair tours are conducted on Tuesdays at 10.30, 11.30 and 13.45 hrs.

Sixty lords sat on each side of the House, with the king's representative, the viceroy, on a throne at the end.

Furnishing with history

The House of Lords' tapestries are original, dating from 1733. One depicts the siege of Londonderry, and another the Glorious Battle of the Boyne. Over the 1748 fireplace is King Billy. The beautiful woodwork is all Irish oak.

The Dublin-made chandelier originally hung in the Commons. It was made for beeswax candles; was taken down and stored when gas lighting was introduced; and was then reassembled when electricity took over. The original chandelier from the Lords now hangs in the Examination Hall of Trinity College.

On your way out, peek into the main banking hall, which used to be the House of Commons. Look at the beautiful woodwork of the counters, and the gorgeous ceiling. Cash exchange is in another department.

Just around the corner in Foster Place is the Bank of Ireland's Arts Centre which opened in November 1995. Originally known as The Armory, the building was attached to the Parliament. Occasional concerts are given, and upstairs is a museum devoted to the history of banking.

Also upstairs is the mace of the Irish House of Commons. An audio-visual display re-enacts the final impassioned debate when the Commons voted for the Act of Union and the demise of their own Irish Parliament.

Speaker Foster held on to the mace, and passed it on to his descendants. In 1937 it was bought back by the Bank of Ireland so that it could return to the former Parliament buildings.

4.3 Temple Bar

Walk along Dame Street, past the modernistic Central Bank, and take any of the side turnings on the right. *See map, fig. 18.* Known as Temple Bar, the riverside area between the Bank of Ireland and Christ Church Cathedral is a successful experiment in urban renewal.

Where style is trendy

This run-down 18th-century commercial district, scheduled for the bulldozer, has been restored to new life as a 'Left Bank' style of arts quarter, full of trendy restaurants, antique dealers, second-hand and antiquarian bookshops, pubs and night clubs.

The annual calendar is packed with special events, from a Blues Festival to open-air performance of the 'Messiah' – a reminder that in 1742 Handel conducted the world premiere of his work at a venue in Fishamble Street.

Opposite the Information Centre at Curved Street is the ARTHOUSE Multimedia Centre for the Arts. Open Mon-Fri 10-13 and 14-17.30 hrs.

The entire Temple Bar area has a quirky atmosphere and pedestrians have priority. Traffic does not flow, but merely inches along. It's certainly worth a visit, day or night – preferably both.

Walk free across Ha'penny Bridge

Down Crown Alley, the Merchant's Arch leads directly to Ha'penny Bridge. This charming pedestrian bridge, erected in 1816, takes its name from the original toll cost of walking across. It offers a classic view of riverside Dublin, and pedestrians no longer have to pay.

Chapter Five
The Grafton Street area

5.1 Grafton Street

With the development of Grafton Street from 1708, and Dawson Street from 1723, the area running from College Green to St Stephen's Green became a fashionable Georgian residential district. *See map, fig. 23.*

Now pedestrianized, it has long since changed into Dublin's leading shopping zone, together with the side turnings and parallel streets. Even after shop closing time, the area still remains lively until late, thanks to the numerous popular pubs. Some of these have close links with literary characters, many of whom like Brendan Behan were "drinkers with a writing problem."

Maybe it's not quite literature, but the song in praise of Molly Malone is immortalized in a bronze statue of the lady, at the top end of Grafton Street. Wheeling a barrow with three rope baskets of fish, cockles and mussels, the Molly Malone sculpture was donated to the city in 1988 by the Jury's Hotel group.

Molly Malone originally graced the city with her presence during the mid-18th century. According to some reports, she sold fish by day and entertained gentlemen by night. Hence the grief at her sad death.

Ever since Molly and her assets have been displayed so liberally, she has acquired various names for herself: 'The Dish with the Fish' or 'The Tart with the Cart', to quote a couple.

Bewley's

Curiously there are no pubs on Grafton Street itself. Instead the most famous meeting-place is a traditional teashop called Bewley's.

The atmosphere is delightful, with stained glass windows and Oriental wallpaper which was trendy when this teashop opened in the 1920s. In winter there's an old-fashioned fire with live coals.

Waitresses are dressed in Victorian black and white, with the traditional head-dress like the frilly paper that goes around a birthday cake. Bewley's is always packed, and you can hardly hear the clatter of the teacups for all the talking, talking, talking…

Upstairs, the Museum Restaurant is somewhat quieter, and displays equipment from a 19th-century bakery and items of merchant tea and coffee interest. The staff ring up cash sales on a mechanical till from the twenties.

Old boys of Whyte's Academy

This branch of Bewley's stands on the site of a Georgian-era school called Whyte's Academy, which flourished from 1758 till 1824. Among the distinguished pupils listed on the honours board was Arthur Wellesey, who later became the Duke of Wellington.

A still earlier scholar was Richard Brinsley Sheridan, who became the most famous and prolific playwright of the late 18th century.

Another pupil to make his mark was Thomas Moore, the poet and classics scholar, who in 1794 was one of the first-ever Catholic students admitted to Trinity College. Moore produced an ever-popular series of *Irish Melodies*.

He was also a great friend of Sheridan and Lord Byron. When Byron died, he left Moore part of his library, which is housed today in the Royal Irish Academy in Dawson Street.

Another of Moore's friends and fellow-students was Robert Emmet, the younger brother of one of the revolutionaries of 1798. Robert Emmet led a small rebellion himself in 1803, but was captured and executed. Because he was only 25, a Trinity student, and was handsome and had a sweetheart, he became one of Ireland's heroes, especially famed for a much-quoted speech from the dock.

Literature on Duke Street

Just around the corner in Duke Street are two more stops on the literary trail. The Duke Pub is the starting point most evenings for a Literary Pub Crawl. This pub also had links with the Hothouse Flowers, on Dublin's Rock 'n Stroll music trail.

Opposite is Davy Byrne's, where nobody raises an eyebrow if you order a glass of burgundy and a Gorgonzola cheese sandwich. They'll just know you are a follower of the James Joyce saga, ordering the same as Leopold Bloom when he stopped here for sustenance on June 16, 1904.

In another side turning called Harry Street is McDaid's, renowned for its links with Brendan Behan and his poet rival, Patrick Kavanagh, and the comic novelist Flann O'Brien, who wrote books such as *The Third Policeman*. It's still a popular locale for a Bohemian lifestyle wrapped around alcohol and endless talk.

5.2 Powerscourt Townhouse

For a shopping centre with a difference, go down the alley called Johnsons Court, by the side of Bewley's cafe, into Clarendon Street. Powerscourt Townhouse is a beautiful conversion of one of Dublin's greatest Georgian mansions into a unique shopping centre, with live piano music and choice of nine cafes or restaurants.

The house was built for Lord Powerscourt in 1774, using granite hauled from the family estate in County Wicklow. With the front entrance at 59 South William Street, no expense was spared.

Superb plaster

The hall and staircase was decorated with stucco work in rococo style, done by leading craftsmen. The main reception rooms on the first floor were decorated by Michael Stapleton in the new Adamesque style.

During the 19th century, the house was bought by the Government, who added three groups of buildings around the courtyard for use as a stamp office. Later the complex was sold off to other commercial interests and went steadily downhill.

When the developers bought the site in 1979, it had gone very shabby. But in the conversion to a modern shopping centre, the new owners preserved all the fine old woodwork and restored the plaster ceilings to their original splendour.

The central courtyard was initially the stables area, now occupied by eating places and a stage for lunchtime concerts, jazz concerts and chamber music recitals. There are trendy boutiques and high-grade craft shops.

A shop on the first floor selling Finnish and Italian furnishings was formerly the main dining room with a superb ceiling. The ballroom with a coloured ceiling is now a commercial art gallery. *(See chapter 12 for shoppping details).*

Dublin Civic Museum

Take the South William Street exit from the Powerhouse, and the Civic Museum is only two doors away, at no. 58.

There's a somewhat pitted head of Nelson, whose column in O'Connell Street was blown up in 1966 to mark the 50th anniversary of the Easter Rising; and there's an array of cast-iron manhole covers. But permanent exhibits are often stored away while a temporary show is put on.

The somewhat dusty collection is worth a quick ten minutes if you're passing by. But don't make a big detour for this modest museum.

Open Tue-Sat 10-18 hrs; Sun 11-14 hrs. Entrance free.

Facing the wall and railings of Trinity College, Nassau Street leads past a number of stores that display modern Irish craft products.

Just past the Trinity College railings was formerly the site of Finn's Hotel. For those making a James Joyce pilgrimage, this is hallowed territory. A young lady called Lorna Barnacle worked at Finn's Hotel as a chambermaid. Following upon an impulsive proposal, Lorna eloped with Joyce and became his lifelong companion and ultimately his wife.

Close by, at 1 Lincoln Place, Sweny's Pharmacy is another cherished site where Leopold Bloom – the lead character in Joyce's novel – bought a cake of lemon-scented soap. The shop interior is preserved in every detail, just like in 1904, and the lemon soap still finds a ready sale.

Parallel to Grafton Street is Dawson Street, which was developed in the early Georgian period. The street is named after Joshua Dawson, a property speculator of the early 18th century. In 1710, Dawson built his own house there, but in 1715 he sold it to Dublin Corporation to become the Mansion House, the official residence of Dublin's Mayor. *See map, fig. 30.*

The Lord Mayor of Dublin is not directly elected. He is an elected city councillor, but the council themselves choose the Lord Mayor from amongst their own membership. His position is held for 12 months only, starting from July 1 each year.

The mayor's official car has a registration number of D 1. Three burning castles in the city's coat of arms relate to acts of retaliation against marauders from the hills.

Although the Mansion House is early Georgian, the decoration is 19th century. That is likewise true of St Anne's Church (also on Dawson Street) – a church built in 1720, with an elaborate 19th century facade.

Kildare Street

Molesworth Street leads past antique stores and the Freemasons' Hall into Kildare Street, facing Leinster House. The Freemasons' Hall is the world's second oldest Grand Lodge, dating from 1725 – the first having been inaugurated in London eight years earlier. Visits are possible between mid-June and August.

Kildare Street is lined with stately institutions: the National Museum *(see details in chapter 9)*, the National Library, the Royal College of Physicians and the former Kildare Street Club.

5.4 St Stephen's Green

Measuring about a quarter mile each side, St Stephen's Green reflects the history and growth of Dublin over past centuries. *See map, fig. 28.*

During the 13th century, the area was common land, open for cattle grazing by local residents. In 1635 a local law was passed, to ensure that the Green should remain in common ownership for the enjoyment of all citizens. The same ordinance also applied to College Green and other open spaces.

Even so, in 1663 the municipality rented out 30 acres of the remaining 57 acres of St Stephen's Green, and the common land was enclosed from 1678.

With the development of Grafton Street and then Dawson Street in the early 18th century, plots of land around the Green soared in value and were acquired by wealthy people for building high-grade housing.

Some of those buildings still face onto the Green. During that time – from mid-17th century onwards – the Green was occasionally used for public hangings. By 1814 the Green had become an unpleasant mess, with blocked ditches and stagnant water. So the City Council rented the Green to the surrounding householders for their private use, railed off from the public.

Dublin's breathing space

Finally, in the 1870s, the Guinness family bought up the rights of all the key-holders, and paid for conversion of the Green into a pleasant public park. Extensive landscaping included a three-acre lake with a cascade and waterfowl. This is the Victorian-style park which survives today.

The Green is now the responsibility of the Office of Public Works, which also undertakes general protection of Ireland's wildlife, under the Wildlife Act of 1976. But the great popularity of St Stephen's Green ensures that the numerous waterfowl can always expect year-round handouts of breadcrumbs.

The entrance nearest to Grafton Street is through a triumphal arch in memory of the officers, NCO's and men of the Royal Dublin Fusiliers who fell at Ladysmith during the South African War of 1899-1900. There are numerous other monuments around the paths and gardens, including a Henry Moore sculpture in the Yeats memorial garden.

In the northeast corner is a statue of Theobald Wolfe Tone, who led a rebellion in 1798. A friend of Napoleon, he could be regarded as Ireland's first Republican.

Close by is a monument to the Great Hunger, the Potato Famine of 1845-47. By the Leeson Street gate are 'The Three Graces', a bronze group donated from Germany in recognition of Irish help to refugees after World War I.

The Bernard Shaw House

From St Stephen's Green, it's a 15-minute walk south towards the Grand Canal, to reach 33 Synge Street, where G.B. Shaw was born. In contrast to Dublin's great Georgian mansions, the Shaw House evokes the cosy home life of a music-loving Victorian middle class family. Furnishings are authentic 19th century. *See map, fig. 31.* Open May-Oct, Mon-Sat 10-15 hrs; Sun 11.30-18.00 hrs. Entrance £2.20. By bus: 16, 19 or 22.

Chapter Six
Best of Georgian Dublin

6.1 Looking at Georgian houses

Dublin enjoyed a golden era of expansion during the 18th and early 19th centuries. As described in Chapter 3, the Georgian building developments started in early 18th century, north of the river.

Then, during the 1740s, the developers moved south. A major boost came from the building of Leinster House, completed in 1748 for Lord Kildare who later became the Duke of Leinster. This building must rate as the grandest Georgian mansion in Ireland. *(See fig. 24 – details below).*

Its effect within a 20-year period was to promote the development of Merrion Square and then Fitzwilliam Square as a good address. The fashionable centre of the city moved east, to complete the Georgian transformation. By the end of the 18th century, Dublin was rated as the second greatest city of the British Empire.

The squares were built around a private central park, reserved to the householders around, who paid towards its maintenance. Some squares have become public only in recent times.

From 1757 onwards the Dublin Wide Streets Commission had statutory powers to decide the layout of new streets and squares, and the style of the frontages. The Georgian squares look like terrace developments, but each plot of land was sold individually. However, there was an obligation to keep strictly to the building line and conform to a unity of design.

The Georgian lifestyle

Houses were normally built four storeys high over a basement. Originally, balconies were not allowed. The elegant wrought-iron balconies seen today are mainly 19th century additions.

In these upper-crust Georgian houses, day-to-day living was on the hall floor. Here the dining room was located, and a room where the ladies would do their embroidery and play cards. Servants were in the basement.

Entertaining was always on the first floor, which had the most decorative ceilings, the best paintings and the finest furniture. The windows were slightly bigger than those on the ground floor, probably to give a better view of the square and its park.

On the top two floors, bedroom windows were smaller, and often were barred for nursery safety. Glass was expensive when these houses were built. To cut the cost, architects calculated that higher floors had fewer obstructions to natural light. So the higher up, the smaller the windows.

Most Georgian houses are of local bricks, though some bricks came from England as ballast. Much of the stone is Portland. There was also great use of local granite on public buildings, which sparkle beautifully when cleaned.

The streets were not paved until the 1840s, long after the houses were built. That's why, on the top steps, just outside the front doors, bootscrapers were essential. These are still a cherished feature outside many houses.

Most of the doors are original, made of Baltic oak. There is great variety of door knockers that are often shaped with human or animal heads. Flanking the doors on either side are pillars supporting a lintel.

Above the lintel is a semi-circular fanlight. Some fanlights are plain, others are very ornate. Even down-to-earth objects like the ornate cast-iron coal hole covers are worth a second look. Several are displayed in the Civic Museum.

Sightseeing after dark

It's also worth wandering round the squares in early evening when office lights are switched on. You can then get a free outside look at many beautiful ceilings with plaster decorations – a great speciality of the Georgian era.

The two sites in Dublin with the most beautiful ceilings are easily accessible: Dublin Castle and Newman House. Belvedere House in Great Denmark Street (*map, fig. 7*) also gets top recommendation for plasterwork by Michael Stapleton.

6.2 Leinster House

James Fitzgerald, the 21st Earl of Kildare, built his great mansion with two main entrances and no back door. *See map, fig. 24.* One entrance looks onto Kildare Street. Another magnificent courtyard opens onto Merrion Square. The Fitzgerald family – the Earls of Kildare and the Dukes of Leinster – remained in occupation until 1814, when the establishment was bought by the Royal Dublin Society.

This prestigious Society had great influence in the city, and was responsible during the 19th century for creation of the major public institutions which were built as extension wings to the central complex of Leinster House.

A bird's-eye view shows an 'H' formation that comprises the National Museum and the National Library in Kildare Street, and the National Gallery and the Natural History Museum (better known to Dublin schoolchildren as 'The Dead Zoo') facing Merrion Square. *(See Chapter 9 for details of the National Museum and the National Gallery).*

After the inauguration of the Irish Free State, the initial meetings of Parliament were held in the Mansion House. Then Leinster House was bought mainly by Irish-American money, and took on its present role as the seat of Parliament, and the offices of the Irish administration.

Dáil and Senate

The Republic of Ireland is a constitutional parliamentary democracy with two Houses. The Lower House is termed the Dáil with 166 elected members. The Upper House or Senate (Seanad) has 60 members, of whom 49 are elected and 11 appointed. The head of government is the Prime Minister, whose Gaelic title means The Chieftain. The elected President serves a 7-year term.

The granite obelisk on Leinster Lawn commemorates Michael Collins and Arthur Griffith who signed the Anglo-Irish Treaty with Lloyd George in 1921. Prince Albert is located at the other end of the lawn. But Queen Victoria was carted off the premises in 1948.

Government Buildings

Adjoining the Natural History Museum, along Upper Merrion Street between Merrion Square and Merrion Row, are Government Buildings which are just over a hundred years old. They were originally built as the Science and Engineering faculties of the Catholic University. That name changed to the National University, and is now better known as UCD – University College Dublin, with at least 12,000 students.

These buildings were taken over by the government. A few years ago the facades were cleaned at a cost of £20 million of taxpayers money, to restore the original gleaming stonework. The Prime Minister at the time was Charles Haughey. When he was finished, Dubliners joked that Chas is short for Charles – so they called this building the Chas Majal.

Across the road, at 24 Merrion Street, was the birthplace of the future Duke of Wellington, who gave his name to the Wellington boot and also did well in battles. In 1829, during his premiership of the British Parliament, the Catholic Emancipation Act was passed –- mainly through pressure exerted by Daniel O'Connell, who lived around the corner at 58 Merrion Square.

Leinster House faces one side of Merrion Square, which is one of the largest and certainly the best preserved of the Georgian developments. *See map, fig. 25.* It was planned in 1762 by John Ensor, the architect who designed Parnell Square across the river. The landowner was Richard Fitzwilliam, sixth Viscount Merrion, who lived here in the 1780s.

A stroll around the square shows that almost every building has an architectural, literary or historical interest. For the past two centuries, Merrion Square has been the address favoured by many of Dublin's social, artistic and political elite.

Oscar Wilde was born at 21 Westland Row, which borders the grounds of Trinity College. But he spent his boyhood at no. 1 Merrion Square. His father was a fashionable eye surgeon who had attended Queen Victoria, and had been given a knighthood.

Oscar Wilde's mother was a fiery radical nationalist, who wrote under the name of 'Speranza' for a newspaper called *The Nation*. This was quite unusual: a well-off Protestant family would normally not wish to rock the boat.

Oscar went to Trinity College. A brilliant student, he defeated his contemporary Edward Carson in a prize to go on to Oxford. There in Oxford he became a leader of the aesthetic movement, very precious in his clothes and opinions.

A great wit, he subsequently enjoyed the greatest possible success as a playwright and novelist. His dramatic fall came as result of a libel action, with his old adversary Edward Carson as crown prosecutor in the trial which sent Oscar Wilde to Reading Gaol.

It was the same Edward Carson who became the leader of the Ulster Unionists in 1912, and who successfully campaigned for the exclusion of the Six Counties from Irish Home Rule.

The best address in Dublin

The buildings around Merrion Square are occupied today by a range of professional institutions, lawyers, architects and the like.

On the south side of the square, number 82 was the residence of William Butler Yeats from 1922 to 1928, when he served as a senator in the Irish Parliament across the road.

From the turn of the century, he was a highly influential figure during the Irish literary revival. Poet, playwright, co-founder of the Abbey Theatre and Nobel prize winner for Literature in 1923, Yeats played a leading role in the Gaelic League which fostered a romantic nationalism.

Daniel O'Connell – 'The Liberator' who gave his name to the main street in the city centre – had his town house at number 58.

By night, a number of houses in Merrion Square are floodlit, including Oscar Wilde's boyhood home. The highlighting brings out vividly many of the Georgian architectural details. Especially attractive is the floodlighting of the Leister House complex of National Gallery, Natural History Museum and the Government Buildings.

6.4 The Fitzwilliam estate

Also floodlit is **Number Twenty Nine**, a fine museum attraction. The floodlighting is appropriate, as the building itself is owned by the Electricity Supply Board. In 1965 that same organisation tore down two dozen Georgian houses along Fitzwilliam Street, to build their headquarter offices. *See map, fig. 26.*

A daytime visit to 29 Lower Fitzwilliam Street, on a corner of Merrick Square, gives a closer idea of the luxurious Georgian lifestyle.

In the basement, a video portrays the daily life of two former occupants – the housekeeper, and the respectable widow lady who owned the property around the end of the 18th century. They talk about their life.

Upstairs, downstairs 200 years ago

The housekeeper's job was to keep the maids in order and also the boy who did the rough jobs. The housekeeper lived in, while the maids lived in a poor part of the city and ran over to work at five in the morning. The widow's life included occasional parties in Dublin Castle, and playing cards with her friends.

Furnishings throughout the house are completely in period, presented by the National Museum of Ireland. The kitchen is specially interesting for its array of very practical utensils: from every size of copper pan to gadgets for crushing salt. The housekeeper's room was in the back basement, where she kept the household keys.

The house did not have running water. A water vendor called every day with his cart, and filled a tank in the basement. In bad weather, when the horse and cart couldn't get round, the maids were sent out with buckets to the town well. The maids were always kept busy, from polishing brasses to carrying hot and cold water and coals up the stairs.

Life upstairs was gracious, with fine furniture and good paintings. Further up was the governess's room, equipped with footwarmers and other practical equipment for keeping warm. There was much use of scented items, because Georgian houses were usually rather smelly.

Open Tue-Sat 10-17 hrs; Sun 14-17 hrs; closed for the two weeks before Christmas. Entrance £2.50.

The Pepper Canister

From the corner of Number Twenty Nine, Mount Street Upper leads to **St Stephen's Church**, built 1824. The locals call it the Pepper Canister, because of the obvious inspiration for its design.

Fitzwilliam Street itself crosses **Lower Baggot Street** – a location which formerly was better known as Gallows Hill. Here, until the late 1850s, petty criminals were executed in public.

Condemned to Australia

If wrongdoers were in sound health, they were transported instead to the penal colonies. Some went to Bermuda, but most were condemned to Tasmania or New South Wales.

Baggot Street today is lined with good restaurants and pubs, including the Baggot Inn where the Moving Hearts rock group made its name in the early 1980s. Further along, Baggot Street changes its name to Merrion Row, where O'Donoghues pub is famed as the original home of The Dubliners. Those two pubs are still packed every night for music. In the Dohenny and Nesbitt pub, the bars are crammed with talkers.

Fitzwilliam Square is the smallest and the last of the Georgian city squares, not finished until 1830, though some houses date from a hundred years earlier. *See map, fig. 27.* Many of the houses are taller than the Georgian terraces around the rest of the city, and some are still used as family homes, rather than being converted into offices. Most buildings have kept their original fanlights, door-knockers and mudscrapers. The central park remains private.

6.5 Around St Stephen's Green

In contrast to Fitzwilliam Square, St Stephen's Green is different in style. St Stephen's Green was the first of the Georgian squares south of the river. Plots of land were actually given to suitable potential residents on condition that they built houses of appropriate quality and size. Many buildings have since been replaced, so there is great variety of architecture.

On the south side is Iveagh House, built partly in 1736 as a town house for the Bishop of Cork and Ross. It was bought in 1856 by the Guinness family, who merged it with the house next door. The ensemble was given to the people of Ireland by Lord Rupert Guinness, the second Earl of Iveagh, in 1939. It is now the Foreign Office.

Newman House

Close by is another merged building – numbers 85 and 86 which comprise Newman House. The name derives from Cardinal Newman who established the Catholic University of Ireland here in 1853, taking over two adjoining 18th-century houses. *See map, fig. 29.*

Among the early lecturers was the Jesuit poet Gerard Manley Hopkins, who taught classics from 1884 until his death in 1889. His room is preserved. Possibly the most famous student at Newman House was James Joyce, whose bust looks across from St Stephen's Green.

The University has long since acquired larger premises to accommodate its 12,000 students. But Newman House has been beautifully restored to the original Georgian elegance, and is open to the public for guided tours.

The plaster decoration is superb. The artists responsible were the Francini Brothers (who also worked in some of the big houses in England) and Robert West (the most famous Irish plaster worker).

Open Tue-Fri 12-17 hrs; Sat 14-17 hrs; Sun 11-14 hrs. Entrance £2.

Next door, the Byzantine style of the University Church, built 1856, is in greatest possible contrast to neighbouring buildings. Also in contrast to Cardinal Newman's austere outlook, the church today is freqently the setting for fashionable Catholic weddings.

Clubland

The north side of St Stephen's Green centres on the Shelbourne Hotel, where the Irish Constitution was drafted in 1922. This side of the Green was formerly known as the Beaux Walk, because of the number of gentlemen's clubs that were located here. They were similar to the clubs in the St. James's area of London. Several still flourish, possibly as the last remaining vestige of the Georgian lifestyle.

Chapter Seven

Medieval Dublin

7.1 The historical background

Dublin is around 1100 years old, founded by Vikings. Before they came, there was no city, although people lived in the area which included some early Christian churches.

These churches had existed from the time of St Patrick, patron saint of Ireland, who introduced Christianity in the fifth century. In fact St Patrick's Cathedral stands on a site where he reputedly baptised converts.

Little churches clustered in the area, and became wealthy from pilgrims who brought gifts during a peaceful golden age from the fifth to the early ninth century.

The treasures of these early Christian churches attracted the Vikings, who arrived in the year 841. For about the first fifty years the Vikings came for plunder, not for settlement. Then, after a decisive battle in December 919, they stayed permanently.

They established a trading colony with a defensive stockade on a ridge overlooking a black or dark pool – *dubh-linn* – where the River Poddle met the Liffey.

The Norsemen came as pagans, but soon intermarried with Irish women. They became Christian, especially after their king was baptised. The settlement flourished as a centre for tanning, weaving and shipbuilding, with occasional trips for trade or loot.

Strongbow takes over

Then came the Anglo-Normans, led by the warrior leader Strongbow in 1170. They defeated the Vikings, and decided that this Norse settlement was the most strategic on the island.

The Irish and the Norsemen were driven from the city, and a new wave of settlers poured in from southwest England, Wales and Bristol.

The original Norse Dublin coincided with today's centre. Then, as the Anglo-Norman city grew bigger, the defensive walls were pushed out. Dublin Castle and the two cathedrals were built.

7.2 Dublin Castle

The Castle dates from the early 13th century on the site developed by the Vikings. *Map, fig. 19.* Dublin Castle operated as a fortress, a prison, Treasury, Courts of Law, and the seat of English administration of Ireland for over 700 years.

Don't expect to find a medieval citadel. It has been greatly rebuilt over the last four centuries, especially following a fire in 1684 which destroyed much of the original structure.

The Record Tower is the only major part that still remains of the original building from 1208.

Of special interest are the foundations of the Powder Tower which formed part of the Norman defensive system. The underground area was found by accident and reveals the stone base on which the Vikings erected their wooden palisade.

Because Viking stonework is such a rare find, archaeologists were intrigued to find exactly how the Vikings managed to hold the rocks together. Analysis showed that their mortar contained a mixture of horsehair, horse blood and eggshells. It was obviously quite effective, being still intact after a thousand years.

From a purely military function, the Castle served more as a viceregal residence from the mid-16th century.

Inside Dublin Castle

The State Apartments are now used for major State receptions, Presidential inaugurations and during Ireland's presidency of the European Community, July to December 1996.

Outside those occasions, the building is open year-round to the public for guided visits: Mon-Fri 10-17 hrs; Sat, Sun and Bank Holidays 14-17 hrs. Entrance £2.

The State Apartments date mainly from the 18th century, Georgian in design and furnishing. There are chandeliers of Waterford crystal, Gobelins tapestries, rich Donegal carpets, Chippendale chairs and superb plasterwork ceilings.

During World War I, the Apartments were used as a military hospital. In the James Connolly Room, the wounded rebel prisoner was nursed until he was taken away for execution. The Queen's Bedroom is still used occasionally by honoured guests. Margaret Thatcher and Nelson Mandela have slept here.

City Hall

Neighbouring the Castle is City Hall, built 1779 and originally intended as the Royal Exchange in this commercial area of Dublin. In front of City Hall are three female statues who represent the crafts of Dublin – woodcraft, stone craft and ironcraft. *See map, fig. 19.*

7.3 St Patrick's Cathedral

Occupying the oldest church site in Ireland, St Patrick's Cathedral was rebuilt in 1191 by John Comyn, the first English archbishop of Dublin; and was then rebuilt again in the following century. *See map, fig. 21.* The Guinness family funded renovation in the 1860s.

The most famous name associated with the Cathedral is Jonathan Swift, Dublin born and educated at Trinity. He wished to enter English politics but settled reluctantly for the church, and was Dean of St Patrick's for his last 32 years.

Swift was born in 1657, when Dublin's population was 9,000. By 1700 it had increased to 70,000. When he died in 1745 it was 140,000.

This wasn't just a natural growth, but the result of landless peasants' flooding in to the city. The great estates were expanding, and landlords were landscaping thousands of acres, tearing people off the land.

The result was dreadful poverty in Dublin, in contrast to the rich life of the Georgian elite. Swift felt deeply about the poor, and expressed his viewpoints in satires which became more vitriolic with increasing age. Fierce indignation was his hallmark.

He is buried in the floor of the cathedral, with his beloved Stella alongside – something quite unusual for a single lady. Another of his loves, named Vanessa, enjoyed less popular support and was buried elsewhere.

This Protestant cathedral is open Mon-Fri 9-18 hrs; Sat 9-17 hrs (Nov-Mar until 16 hrs); Sun 10-16.30 hrs. Entrance £1.20.

Beside the Cathedral is Ireland's first public library, named after its founder Archbishop Narcissus Marsh, who established **Marsh's Library** in 1701. That's where Swift wrote *Gulliver's Travels*. Anyone consulting a rare book was locked into a wired cage.

Open Mon and Wed-Fri 10.00-12.45 and 14-17 hrs; Sat 10.30-12.45. Entrance £1 donation requested.

7.4 Christ Church Cathedral

A wooden church was founded here in 1038 by Sitric Silkbeard, the Danish king of Dublin. From 1172 the cathedral was rebuilt in stone, on orders of the Norman conqueror Strongbow.
See map, fig. 20. His monument in medieval armour replaces the original tomb which was

crushed when the roof fell down in 1562. The north wall has been leaning ever since.

When medieval Dublin was just a tiny city on a hill, Christ Church was the centre of its life for 200 years. Courts of justice were held in the monastery building. Commerce was carried on in the crypt, which today is used for general storage of a variety of monuments, including statues of Charles I and Charles II.

The crypt is Dublin's oldest surviving structure. The last reconstruction of Christ Church was in 1871-78, financed by Henry Roe, a whiskey distiller. The project made him bankrupt.

Open daily 10-17 hrs. Entrance £1 donation. Bus 78A or 50.

7.5 Dublinia

A Senate Hall was built around 1870, attached by a covered bridge to Christ Church Cathedral. Bishops of the Church of Ireland met here every year until 1983. The Senate Hall was then left to become derelict. *See map, fig. 20.*

Since then, The Medieval Trust has converted the building into the Dublinia project which re-creates the period of the city's growth from the arrival of the Anglo-Normans in 1170, until the closure of the monasteries in 1540.

During that time, four different languages were spoken: Latin by the priests, Middle English by the immigrants from southwest Britain, Norman French by the lords and ladies, and Gaelic by the Irish outside town.

Artefacts loaned by the National Museum help create displays of medieval craft workshops, home life, and merchant and leisure activities. An audio-visual presentation fills in the background to medieval life, including hazards like bubonic plague.

Open Apr-Sep daily 10-17 hrs; Oct-Mar Mon-Sat 11-16, Sun 10-16.30 hrs. Entrance £3.95. Bus 78A or 50.

Chapter Eight

Beyond Dublin centre

8.1 The Liberties

During medieval times, areas outside the city walls were known as The Liberties, beyond the city jurisdiction. Beside the Liffey and along Bridge Street to St Patrick's Cathedral formed part of The Liberties. Many refugee French and Dutch Huguenots settled here in the 17th century, and tried to establish industries including cloth weaving.

Complaints from English manufacturers about the competition led to a Parliamentary ruling which blocked woollen exports. The new industry collapsed, and the area never recovered.

Retail trade centres along Thomas Street, but generally it's an area with much poverty and decaying factories. Buses 21A, 78, 78A and 78B pass through The Liberties, en route to the Guinness Brewery, Kilmainham Gaol and the Royal Hospital and its Irish Museum of Modern Art.

8.2 Guinness Hop Store

If you visit the Guinness premises, do not imagine that you will see the brewing of beer! The brewery itself is totally automated, with relatively few people around. *See map, fig. 22.*

Instead, the company offers an exhibition in a converted 19th-century warehouse, with a film on the history of Guinness and the family, and displays that explain how their beer is made.

How to make Guinness

The secret of this famous black beverage with the distinctive white head is the use of roasted barley and malt, which gives it the deep ruby colour. Pure and soft water comes from special reservoirs in the Wicklow Mountains. The only other ingredients are hops and yeast.

From that simple formula, originated by London brewers of the 18th century who supplied the porters of Covent Garden, has grown the Guinness stout which is brewed today in 34 countries.

Entrance to the exhibition costs £2. But effectively you can drink it back, thanks to vouchers for two half pints in the Sample Bar. If you want to be a walking advertisement for Guinness, a shop awaits with tee-shirts and related gear.

Of interest to art lovers, the spacious top floor of the Hop Store is devoted to exhibitions of contemporary artists.

8.3 Kilmainham Hospital

Less than a mile further west is Kilmainham Hospital. This was never a medical institution, but a home for old soldiers like Chelsea Hospital in London. The army retirement home was built in 1684, in similar style to Les Invalides in Paris, with a very large central courtyard and arcades going around. The magnificent building remained in use for old soldiers until 1922, and then housed the Public Record Office.

In 1950 the building was abandoned and lay derelict until 1980. Then, after several years of restoration, it was reopened as the **Irish Museum of Modern Art** – a centre for arts and culture. The collection offers no concessions to the 19th and earlier centuries. On city sightseeing tours, several companies stop here for a leg-stretching exercise, refreshments, or a quick scamper round the galleries.

Open Tue-Sat 10-17.30; Sun 12-17.30 hrs. Entrance free. Buses 79 or 90.

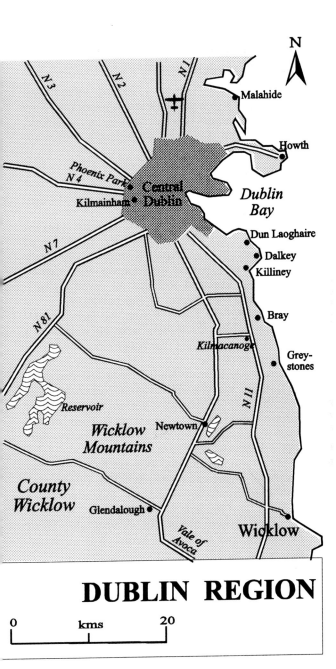

N

Malahide

Howth

Phoenix Park
N 4

Kilmainham

Central
Dublin

*Dublin
Bay*

N3

N2

N1

N7

N 81

Dun Laoghaire

Dalkey

Killiney

Bray

Kilmacanoge

Grey-
stones

N 11

Reservoir

*Wicklow
Mountains*

Newtown

*County
Wicklow*

Glendalough

*Vale
of
Avoca*

Wicklow

DUBLIN REGION

0   kms   20

8.4 Kilmainham Gaol

The prison was built in 1796 and served until 1924, mainly to house political subversives. Now one of the largest untenanted prisons in Europe, it traces grim memories of Ireland's moves towards independence.

The leaders of five rebellions were held here – in 1798, 1803, 1848, 1867 and 1916. Some were executed for treason, others released ultimately to continue in politics.

The events of Easter 1916 had the greatest impact on Irish history. After the surrender of participants in the Easter Rising, ninety death sentences were passed, and fifteen were carried out. Those executed included all seven signatories of the Proclamation of Independence.

Until then, the Easter Rising had lacked popular support. But its leaders were all well-known public figures. When the executions began in Stonebreakers Yard during May 1916, massive protests erupted in Ireland, Britain and America. In London, the War Office grew concerned about how the 200,000 Irishmen serving in the British forces would react when they learned of the death sentences. To avoid possible mutiny, further executions were halted.

There was no mutiny, but the history of Ireland was changed completely. The fifteen men who died by firing squad are honoured today virtually as founders of the Republic. Kilmainham Gaol is now a museum. A visit takes about two hours, and includes an audio-visual presentation and a guided tour through the prison.

Open daily May-Sep 10-18 hrs. Oct-Apr Mon-Fri 13-16 hrs; Sun 13-18 hrs. Entrance £2. Buses 51, 51A, 79.

Fifty thousand Irishmen lost their lives in the British forces during World War I. They, too, are not forgotten. Close by is the national war memorial and its garden, beautifully designed by Sir Edwin Lutyens in the 1930s.

8.5 Phoenix Park

Only two miles from central Dublin is Europe's largest enclosed city park. The 1,752-acre private deer park was established in 1662, and was opened to the public in 1745. Five times the area of London's Hyde Park, it features at least 300 free-range fallow deer, and a Zoo famed for breeding lions. The lion who roars at the opening of every MGM movie was Dublin born.

The President of Ireland lives in Phoenix Park at the so-called White House. From the 1780s until 1922 it was the residence of the Viceroy, the reigning monarch's personal representative. British kings and queens normally stayed in this house during their periodic visits.

Queen Victoria was particularly fond of Dublin, calling four times during her reign. In 1900, she stayed six weeks. Close by is Deerfield House, the home of the US Ambassador,

A large cross commemorates the visit of Pope John Paul II in 1979 – the only occasion when a reigning pope has ever visited Ireland. He celebrated an open-air mass at an altar where the cross now stands. An estimated million people were present, making the papal mass one of the most joyous events which Dublin or its people had ever witnessed.

Another conspicuous monument is the Wellington Testimonial, which commemorates Wellington's victory at Waterloo. When built, it was the world's tallest obelisk, 205 feet high. Why a monument to a British general's victory over a French general in Belgium? Mainly because Wellington was Dublin born, even though he never boasted of the fact. This is probably the only colonial monument in Dublin that wasn't blown up or taken down after Independence.

Notice the style of lighting along the main route through Phoenix Park. This is the only public gas lighting in Dublin.

Buses 10, 25 or 26.

8.6 Malahide Castle

North of Dublin, at the seaside town of Malahide, this splendid castle is over 800 years old and was the home until 1973 of the Talbot family. Now in public ownership, Malahide Castle displays good antique furniture and a range of Irish portraits from the National Gallery collection. Banquets are held in the beautiful Great Hall.

Open Apr-Oct Mon-Fri 10-17 hrs; Sat 11-18; Sun 11.30-18 hrs. Nov-Mar Mon-Fri 10-17 hrs; Sat, Sun & public holidays 14-17 hrs. Entrance £2.85. Bus 42 from Beresford Place (by Dublin's bus station, Busáras) or train from Connolly Station.

Fry Model Railway Museum

Another attraction at Malahide Castle is the model railway, of great technical interest for rail buffs. Every piece was hand crafted by a dedicated railway engineer. Even those who are not normally enthralled by transport will find it fascinating.

The entire system is computerised. The operator presses one button. A single train starts moving, then more and more until some fifty buses, trams, trains and even boats on the River Liffey are moving around.

Open Apr-Sep Mon-Thu 10-18 hrs; Sat 11-18; Sun 2-18 hrs. Jun-Aug also open Fri 10-18 hrs. Oct-Mar Sat, Sun & public holidays 14-17 hrs. Entrance £2.50.

Chapter Nine

Five key museums

If you intend to make a cultural pilgrimage around Dublin, it's worth starting in Parnell Square. *See map, fig. 4.* Three museums are tightly clustered within a minute's walk: Writers Museum for the literary scene, Hugh Lane Gallery for paintings, and the National Wax Museum for a capsule introduction to Irish history.

9.1 Dublin Writers Museum

The Dublin Writers Museum is housed in a restored Georgian town-house, with a splendid staircase to the Gallery of Writers, and original plasterwork in Adam style. On the ground floor, two rooms trace the history of Irish literature through information panels, with display cabinets of memorabilia and first editions.

Irish skill with the spoken and written word goes back at least a thousand years. Ireland had a persistent oral tradition, fostered by its distance from the main centres of medieval 'civilisation'. The written word came only with the arrival of Christianity in the 5th century. Irish storytellers continued for hundreds of years to narrate legends that had been retold over the generations.

With their inherent gift of the gab, storytellers used words not merely as building blocks for sentences, but as ornaments in themselves. The dazzling gift with language has passed down through the centuries, and still survives in Dublin pubs where drinkers are intoxicated with talk.

Words as decoration

There is some parallel with the *Book of Kells* and other medieval manuscripts, in which written words themselves were given elaborate ornament. Never mind the meaning, feel the colour.

In the 18th century, the British theatre was dominated by Irish playwrights. William Congreve – educated at Trinity College, and a fellow student and friend of Swift – was a master of the comedy of manners. George Farquhar followed in the comedy tradition with *The Recruiting Officer* and *The Beaux' Stratagem*.

Oliver Goldsmith – another Trinity graduate – found success with *She Stoops to Conquer*, while his masterpiece *The Vicar of Wakefield* has been translated into more languages than any other 18th-century novel, though he sold it for £60.

Richard Brinsley Sheridan was born in Dublin – his mother a novelist and comedy playwright, his father an actor, theatre manager and author. Sheridan had early success with comedy and farce, and was able to buy out Garrick's share of the Drury Lane Theatre when he was only 25.

Late in the 19th century, Bernard Shaw and then Oscar Wilde came from the literary traditions of Dublin before moving on to capture London. In their individual ways they followed the dazzling Irish tradition of sparkling wit that had a social or satirical bite.

For satire, Ireland's greatest name is Jonathan Swift, the Dean of St Patrick's Cathedral. *Gulliver's Travels* was intended as a political satire, not just a story for children.

Many subsequent writers gave a political or nationalist flavour to their works, especially after the Act of Union of 1801. The novelist Maria Edgeworth portrayed the fashionable society life of the early 19th century, and in *Castle Rackrent* depicted the reckless living which ruined many Irish landlords. Thomas Moore, son of a Dublin grocer, was a prolific writer of lyrics and was regarded as the national poet of Ireland.

From *Dracula* to Nobel prizewinning

On a somewhat different plane, Abraham Stoker published *Dracula* in 1897, full of shock, horror and melodrama. 'Bram' Stoker lived at 30 Kildare Street, opposite the National Museum.

The Nobel Prize poet, William Butler Yeats, was deeply inspired by the Gaelic movement and was a co-founder of the Irish National Theatre Company.

Looking to Irish roots, the Abbey Theatre has fostered local writers, and staged classics by John Millington Synge and Sean O'Casey which caused riots at their first performances. *The Playboy of the Western World* is in the great Irish comic tradition of a bubbling enthusiasm for words.

The tradition moves on to Nobel Prizewinner Samuel Beckett, though in fact he left Ireland in 1931, and returned only from time to time. In more recent decades, Brendan Behan has become the stuff of legend, leaving rich oral memories in dozens of Dublin pubs.

The oral storytelling tradition also finds its 20th-century equivalent in the short story. Elizabeth Bowen, Liam O'Flaherty, Frank O'Connor and Sean O'Faolain are all part of the rich history of Dublin writers.

Possibly the greatest and most controversial of Dublin's 20th-century writers is James Joyce. He spent his formative first 22 years in Dublin, followed by 36 years in Trieste, Zurich and Paris. But he wrote only about Dublin, in such detail that he claimed that if the city were ever destroyed, it could be entirely rebuilt from his works.

Many dedicated admirers of *Ulysses* take pleasure in following in the steps of Leopold Bloom, whose odyssey around Dublin on June 16, 1904 is described so minutely. On that anniversary date every year, enthusiasts come specially to Dublin to celebrate Bloomsday in period dress and with impromptu readings.

Acceptance came late

During the lifetime of Joyce, *Ulysses* remained an underground masterpiece – never officially banned in Dublin, but not generally accepted till much later. Today there are even plaques in the pavement with quotes from the book, along part of Leopold Bloom's fictional route from Abbey Street to Kildare Street.

The Writers Museum displays a piano bought by James Joyce during his time in Trieste, when he was earning barely enough to feed his family.

Open Mon-Sat 10-17 hrs; Sun and public holidays 11.30-18.00. In Jun-Aug there is late opening Mon-Fri till 19 hrs. Entry £2.75. There are reduced-rate combined tickets that also include the Shaw Birthplace at 33 Synge Street, and/or the James Joyce Tower and Museum at Sandycove near Dun Laoghaire.

9.2 Hugh Lane Gallery

The nucleus of the art treasures in this gallery is part of a magnificent collection of French Impressionist paintings, donated by Sir Hugh Lane.

This was Ireland's first gallery of modern art, and is the second largest public collection after the National Gallery of Ireland. When Sir Hugh died in the sinking of the Lusitania in 1915, an unsigned codicil to his will resulted in 50 years of legal battles with London's National Gallery over possession of the pictures. The Lane Bequest is now shared between the two galleries.

The collection includes works by Degas, Manet, Vuillard and Pierre Bonnard; and into the 20th century with Maurice de Vlaminck and Georges Rouault. There are paintings by Constable, Burne Jones, Augustus John, Walter Sickert and Whistler. Twentieth-century Irish artists are well represented, and the gallery also displays some contemporary stained glass.

Open Tue-Fri 9.30-18.00 hrs; Sat 9.30-17.00; Sun 11-16 hrs. Entrance free.

For anyone interested in Irish history and politics, it's worth visiting the Wax Museum at Granby Row, just around the corner from Parnell Square. *See map, fig. 5.* Historical scenes with a background narrative give the Irish viewpoint on the uprisings that finally led to Independence.

In the 1790s, for instance, Wolfe Tone formed a United Irishmen movement, dedicated to making Ireland an independent republic. To support the cause, he encouraged the French to launch an invasion of Ireland during the Napoleonic Wars. A display shows him ready to set sail aboard a French ship for an attack that was thwarted by bad weather at Bantry Bay off the south coast.

In 1798 a second attempt was intercepted by the British Navy off the Donegal coast. Tone was captured and brought to Dublin. He took his own life, rather than face hanging as a traitor.

In the next scene, the youthful Robert Emmet is on trial for his life in a Dublin courtroom, following the failure of a revolt in 1803. His speech from the dock was one of the most inspiring pieces of Irish patriotic oratory. "When my country takes her place among the nations of the earth, then and not till then, let my epitaph be written."

There are similar dramatic scenes from the lives of Daniel O'Connell 'The Liberator', Michael Davitt of the Land League, Charles Parnell, and the leaders of the Easter Rising of 1916.

For a family audience there's a Chamber of Horrors and coverage of Mega-Stars and Irish personalities of sport, TV and music. Something different: the Pope Mobile used by Pope John Paul II on his visit to Dublin in 1979; also the 'Last Supper' in wax.

However, don't expect a Madame Tussaud's.

Open Mon-Sat 10.00-17.30; Sun 12.00-17.30 hrs. Entrance £3.50.

Soon after its foundation in 1785, a museum committee was formed to promote all antiquarian pursuits. Hence, from the beginning, Irish prehistoric ornaments have occupied an important place in the national collection.

Among the highlights of Ireland's Stone and Bronze Ages, there are superb golden necklaces, dress and sleeve fasteners and bracelets. Earrings are made from gold nuggets. The museum's collection of Bronze Age gold is the finest in Western Europe. It makes one drool.

Closer to modern Dublin is Viking Age Ireland, which shows the lifestyle of Dubliners between 800 and 1000 AD, and the impact of the Viking invasions on the rural economy and on the Irish church.

The Treasury holds the masterpieces of early medieval art, spanning the period from the end of the Bronze Age to the 15th century AD. It is divided into three main areas: prehistoric iron age objects, an audio-visual room, and a gallery displaying the late Celtic and medieval treasures, for which the National Museum is famous.

Most of the remaining exhibitions demonstrate Irish skills in craft products: Dublin engraved glass, silver, ceramics, textiles and tapestries. A collection of musical instruments is rich in Irish harps.

Twentieth-century history

The historical gallery entitled 'The Road to Independence' concentrates on the period 1900-1921, with special reference to the events and personalities of Easter week, 1916. A 12-minute video, based on contemporary film, gives an account of the Rising.

During those events, in the first world war, between 150 and 200 thousand Irish volunteers joined the British Army. They were encouraged by a massive recruiting drive, and also by claims that they were fighting for the freedom of small nations. The Irish regiments suffered huge casualties on several fronts, especially on the Somme, and at Gallipoli.

The National Museum collections will ultimately move to Collins Barracks, near Phoenix Park. Meanwhile the entrance is in Kildare Street, alongside Leinster House. Open Tue-Sat 10-17 hrs; Sun 14-17 hrs. Entrance free.

9.5 National Gallery of Ireland

Founded in 1854, the gallery houses the national collection of European master paintings from the 14th to the 20th centuries, including works by Fra Angelico, Goya, Rubens and Breughel. All the major European schools since the Renaissance are represented, together with a comprehensive collection of the better known Irish artists.

In the forecourt is a statue of George Bernard Shaw, who bequeathed royalties from his published works to the gallery in thanks for the education he received here as a boy.

With a new extension opened in spring 1996, the entire gallery has been re-hung to display more of the pictures which formerly were held in store.

The new facilities at the gallery include state-of-the-art air conditioning and lighting, and an audio guide system available for hire with a CD Rom to give information about most of the paintings on display. An exciting programme of temporary exhibitions is promised.

Open Mon-St 10-17.30 hrs; Thu late closing at 20.30; Sun 14-17 hrs. *See map, fig. 24.* Entrance free, but a donation is appreciated.

Chapter Ten

South coast to Wicklow

10.1 Along the coast

Spreading around Dublin Bay are several seaside dormitory suburbs, linked by a coastal highway that continues south to Bray and the beautyspots of the Wicklow Mountains.

The coastal strip is also served by DART – the Dublin Area Rapid Transport system. It's the only electrified line in Ireland, and runs from Howth on the north side of Dublin, through central Dublin to Bray in the south. Catch the train at Tara Street Station or Pearse Station. It takes 40 minutes to Bray, or 25 minutes to Dalkey.

Booterstown combines fine views with a bird sanctuary that's a mixture of salt and fresh water marsh, a favourite haunt of ornithologists. The singer, John MacCormack, lived here.

On the right is **Blackrock College**, a Catholic institution famed for rugby. Eamon de Valera was a pupil and later taught at the college, subsequently becoming Prime Minister and afterwards President of Ireland. Another pupil of international stature was Bob Geldof.

Along the coast are wide open stretches that look more like mudflats than sand, with an occasional Martello Tower looking across the bay. Seventy of these lookout towers were built in 1804 along the east coast, in response to the possibility of a Napoleonic invasion.

The harbour of **Dun Laoghaire** (pronounced Dunleary) took forty years to complete during the 19th century, and covers 250 acres. The port was called Kingstown in honour of King George IV until 1921. It continues to serve as a main ferry terminal, and now features crossings from Holyhead in less than two hours aboard Stena Line's high speed superferry.

The east pier is a popular place for a stroll. It was a great tradition for Irish people to wave goodbye to the mail-boat on which their friends or relatives were emigrating, never to return.

Several elite Yacht Clubs are located here, including the Royal Irish and the Royal Saint George. The principal hotel is the Royal Marine. Presumably this Victorian-style resort hasn't yet fully realised that Ireland is now a Republic.

The panther that wasn't there

At Sandycove is the most famous of the Martello Towers, briefly occupied by James Joyce until pistol shots at a non-existent black panther persuaded him to leave hurriedly.

The tower is setting for the opening chapter of *Ulysses*, and is now the **James Joyce Museum**, with the gun platform and living room preserved exactly as described in the book.

Open only in summer, Apr-Oct, Mon-Sat 10-17 hrs; Sun 14-18 hrs. Entrance £2.20.

Bernard Shaw lived here

The seaside route continues past Bulloch Harbour. The village of **Dalkey**, where Bernard Shaw lived for a while, has a Queen's pub and a King's Inn. From the tiny harbour of Coliemore, summer boat trips operate to Dalkey Island offshore. It's a bird sanctuary which also has the ruins of an 8th-century Benedictine church, a Martello tower and a herd of goats.

The coastal scenery becomes still more attractive, wooded and hilly, closer to Wicklow Mountains. **Killiney Bay** is specially beautiful, often compared to the Bay of Naples but without the risk of sunstroke.

10.2 County Wicklow

Just over the Wicklow border, **Bray** is the largest seaside resort on the east coast, overlooked by 793-ft Bray Head. Traditional in style, Bray has a bandstand and a mile-long promenade.

County Wicklow is known as the Garden of Ireland, with dramatic coastal scenery. In the beautiful mountains are fine stands of trees.

En route to Glendalough, many tour groups stop at Kilmacanogue where a magnificent 19th-century arboretum was developed by the Jameson family of whiskey fame.

The family mansion became a hotel which burnt down. The site is now a restaurant, and a sales outlet for classic handwoven garments and machine-made knitwear. But the unique trees are untouched.

Glendalough

The sightseeing highlight of the Wicklow Mountains, Glendalough is famed for the historic and archaeological interest of its ruined cathedral – part of a monastic settlement founded by St Kevin in the 6th century.

After flourishing for 800 years, this great medieval seat of learning was burnt and abandoned in 1398 during warfare between the Normans and the local chiefs.

The steep wooded hills that hem in the valley offer beautiful views of two lakes. Scattered among the trees are more ruins of the monastic buildings, which until 600 years ago housed students from all Europe.

Chapter Eleven

Dublin by night

Up-to-date listings of galleries, exhibitions, pubs, clubs, restaurants, theatres and every other nightlife event and activity are published by a fortnightly magazine called *In Dublin*. It is excellent value for £1.50, and is worth buying at any newsagent immediately you arrive. You can then plan evening activities precisely in line with your personal interests.

Regrettably the magazine is not on sale in Britain. But all the current listings are available on the Internet. Go to http://www.indublin.ie/, and you can download detailed information, day by day across the magazine's 14-day coverage, including reviews of current stage plays and comments on the nightlife scene.

Somewhat less comprehensive, but free, is the *Dublin Event Guide*, also published fortnightly and available at hotel desks or from the Dublin Tourism Centre in Suffolk Street. An Internet version is promised on http://www. events.homenet.ie/.

Another free listings publication is *Where Dublin*, published on a seasonal basis.

11.1 Theatres

A visit to one or other of Dublin's world-famous theatres – the Abbey, or the Gate – can be an enduring memory. Phone ahead for programme details, and to reserve seats by credit card.

Abbey – Lower Abbey Street. As the National Theatre, concentrates on plays by Irish writers. Typical prices are £10 and £12.50; Mondays £7.50; matinees and previews £6. Tel: 878 7222.

Gaiety – South King Street. Opera and stage shows. Tel: 677 1717.

Gate – Cavendish Row, corner of Parnell Square. Plays by international writers. Tickets £11 and £13, previews £9. Tel: 874 4045.

Olympia - 72 Dame Street, was built 1879 and still looks Victorian. It offers a varied programme from musicals and ballet, to late night rock after the main show. Tel: 677 7744.

Peacock – In The Abbey basement, an associated theatre specialising in more experimental works. Tel: 878 7222.

11.2 Eating out

Ireland gets top marks for food. Even a reasonably-priced menu can include trump cards like trout, salmon or turkey. The visitor can revel in good eating, without pain on the pocket. Many hotels and restaurants offer special-value tourist menus at fixed prices.

More restaurants offer international cuisine than traditional Irish. But it's worth searching the menus for Irish specialities like stuffed turkey and ham with cranberries, or even Irish stew.

With proximity to the sea, there is good choice of freshly landed seafood. However, despite the popularity of Molly Malone, it's hard to find cockles and mussels on the menu, though the Shelbourne Hotel can oblige with 'Molly Malone's fresh cockles and mussels' for £6.25. They also offer an Irish stew for £7.

Numerous restaurants are clustered in the Temple Bar area, in the side turnings off Grafton Street, and along Baggot Street.

The listings publications give extensive coverage to the food scene, so that you can easily choose from the great variety: Irish, Continental,

Asian, American, Middle Eastern or Vegetarian. **In Dublin**, for instance, describes over 250 eating places, giving an idea of the style of restaurant, and the price-range to expect.

To illustrate the range, here's a short list of central restaurants recommended by Thomson's on-the-spot staff.

Trocadero, 3 St Andrew's Street, near Dublin Tourist Centre. Go here for the atmosphere, young and lively. Pre-theatre dinners are served from 6 p.m., and after-show suppers until midnight. International cuisine, with vegetarian available. Tel: 677 5545.

Tosca, 20 Suffolk Street. From the name, obviously Italian cuisine, very good on pasta dishes, with modern art decor around the walls. Tel: 679 6744.

La Stampa, 35 Dawson St, facing the Mansion House. French food in a beautiful up-market setting. Tel: 677 8611.

QV2, 14/15 St Andrew's Street. Medium priced, and handy for lunch, and before or after theatre with friendly service. Tel: 677 3363.

Pasta Fresca, Chatham Court, Chatham Street – close to the St Stephen's Green end of Grafton St. Open for breakfast from 8 a.m., popular all day with reasonable prices. Tel: 679 2402.

Nico's, 53 Dame St, near the Central Bank. Italian cuisine, but some Irish, with piano accompaniment. Tel: 677 3062.

Restaurant Patrick Guilbaud, 46 James Place, off Baggot Street. Rated as Dublin's top French restaurant, outstanding for seafood. Elegant and pricey. Tel: 676 4192.

Fitzers Cafés, 51 Dawson St and also at the National Gallery, and at 24 Upper Baggot Street. A multi-location group offering good-value meals with a wide international flavour.

Baton Rouge, 119 St Stephen's Green. Creole cuisine in Louisiana style, and Sunday brunch with jazz. Tel: 475 2255.

11.3 The pub scene

If you ask for a Guinness the barman will automatically pull a pint. If you order "a glass of Guinness" that means half a pint – a measure used mainly for the ladies. In the macho world of the Irish, men drink only pints.

Popular pubs become very crowded, even before shops and offices are officially closed. The more rambling style of pubs have cosy little snugs which permit more privacy than in the main bars. Go later, and it's standing room only.

Some pubs specialise in music, others in talk – politics, racing, theatre, the day's news, writing, or just plain gossip. The listings publications give clues to the current scene, especially on what style of music to expect at different pubs.

Extremely popular is the **Literary Pub Crawl**, – meeting 7.30 p.m. at Duke's Pub on Duke Street, between Dawson and Grafton Streets. If you have some basic familiarity with the works of James Joyce, Brendan Behan, Oscar Wilde, Samuel Beckett and other notorious literary characters associated with Dublin, then it's a most enjoyable evening, with pauses at various localities (mostly pubs) associated with these authors.

Each group is led by two professional actors, who relate stories and play brief scenes. Plenty of good laughs help give excellent value for the £6 price of the tour. It can inspire you to return with renewed interest to the authors mentioned.

Irish Hooley Nights

Some pubs combine traditional food with a programme of live music and dance. Most of these old-time taverns are 200 years old or more, with stone flag or wooden floors, and crackling log fires on chilly nights.

Set and Irish dancing involves audience participation. Diners can join in the singing of rebel songs, and dance jigs and reels on the sawdust floor. Several Dublin city establishments feature these Hooley Nights:

Pier 32 Pub at 32 Upper Pembroke Street. Tel: 676 1494.

Castle Inn at 5 Lord Edward St. Tel: 478 0663.

Kitty O'Shea's at 23 Grand Canal St Upper - a trendy Hooley Pub venue. Tel: 660 9965.

Hole in the Wall beside Phoenix Park, where they also feature a carvery lunch daily, with traditional ballads at Sunday lunchtime. Tel: 838 9491.

Another dozen Hooley Pubs are located in Dublin County, within 20 minutes of the city centre. Entertainment-only packages are available, to include one drink, at around £6 to £8 per person; or you can choose a package with a full Irish menu. To save a lot of phoning around, a central reservations office can give individual details on phone 688-8622.

A traditional **Irish Musical Pub Crawl** starts every night except Friday from Oliver St John Gogarty's at 57 Fleet Street in Temple Bar. Led by a professional musician, the tour visits McDaids and The Clarendon, and ends at O'Donoghue's in Merrion Row, where The Dubliners first made their name.

Pub crawls for self-starters

An alternative is to compile your own pub crawl. Here's a listing across several central areas, where you can look in at tavern after tavern, staying a while at whichever takes your fancy.

Most of the suggested pubs feature music either nightly, or on an occasional basis. It could be worth checking first with a few phone calls. Some pubs are included because of their special atmosphere or for their literary associations.

Many of the pubs serve food, mostly traditional Irish rather than anything fancy. But some have quite serious restaurants, with a menu at the entrance so that you can assess the range.

Grafton Street area

Here is Dublin's prime drinking zone, with dozens of pubs within a few minutes' walk. Curiously there are no pubs on Grafton Street itself, though they flourish in the little side turnings, and in the parallel streets from Great Georges Street South to Dawson Street; and up to Dame Street.

Dame Tavern, 18 Dame Court. Pub grub. Tel: 679 3426.

Molly Malones Tavern, Great Georges St South/ Dame Court. A traditional and lively Irish music pub. Pub grub.

The George Bar, 89 South Great Georges St. Bistro. Tel: 478 2983.

The Old Stand, 37 Exchequeur St. Pub grub till 9 p.m. "The Old Stand, and everyone else sits down." Many literary links. Tel: 677 7220.

The International Bar, 23 Wicklow St. Live music, and comedy. Pub grub. Tel: 677 9250.

Judge Roy Beans, Nassau St. Pub grub.

The Clarendon, 32 Clarendon St. A popular music pub. Pub grub. Tel: 679 2909.

McDaids, 3 Harry St. Top-rated literary pub, with regular blues and jazz. Young atmosphere. Pub grub. Tel: 679 4395.

Bruxelles, 7 Harry St. Pub grub. Tel: 677 5362.

The Duke, 8/9 Duke St. No music, but great literary associations; starting point of the Literary Pub Crawl. Irish food. Tel: 679 9553.

Temple Bar area

From O'Connell Bridge to Grattan Bridge, the swinging and trendy Temple Bar area has brought new vitality to the Dublin scene, thanks to lively restoration of a former derelict zone.

The Harp, O'Connell Bridge. Pub grub. Tel: 677 7835.

The Fleet Bar, 28 Fleet St. Pub grub. Tel: 679 8392.

Buskers, in the Temple Bar Hotel, Fleet St. Pub grub.

Oliver St John Gogarty, 24/25 Fleet St. Traditional Irish music nightly, starting point for a Musical Pub Crawl every night except Fri at 7.30. Irish menu; Sunday brunch. Tel: 671 1822.

Auld Dubliner, 24 Temple Bar. One of the oldest bars in the area. Pub grub. Tel: 677 0527.

Eamonn Doran's, 3A Crown Alley, Temple Bar. Live bands and traditional Irish music. DJ after midnight, and food till 2 a.m. Tel: 679 9114.

Ha'Penny Bridge Inn, 42 Wellington Quay. Pub grub. Tel: 677 0616.

The Norseman, Essex St East. A friendly traditional pub with live music on Sun nights. Pub grub.

Fitzsimons Bar & Restaurant, Essex Street East. Traditional Irish music and set dancing with banjo, fiddle, uileann pipes, tin whistle and bodhrán. Sunday brunch. Tel: 677 9315.

Rumpoles Lounge, 18 Parliament St. A favourite haunt of theatre people, with live blues Wed and Thu. Tel: 679 9202.

The Oak Bar, 81 Dame St. Pub grub. Tel: 677 2504.

Parliament Inn, 27 Parliament St. A gay and lesbian meeting point. Pub grub.

Kildare St, Merrion Row & Baggott St area

Kildare Bar, Kildare St. Pub grub.

Pink Elephant, Frederick St.

O'Donoghue's, 15 Merrion Row. Usually very crowded, with music trying to make itself heard above the babble. Here was launch-pad of The Dubliners. Pub grub. Tel: 676 2807.

Foley's, Merrion Row.

Doheny and Nesbitt, 5 Baggot St Lower. A great place for stand-up talk, with music sometimes. Pub grub. Tel: 676 2945.

Baggot Inn, 143 Baggot St. Live music nightly. The Irish home of rock, where the Moving Hearts played from 1981. Pub grub. Tel: 676 1430.

West of St Stephen's Green to Aungier Street

Sinnotts Bar, King Street South. Traditional Irish music nightly. Decorated with pictures of famous writers of the last two centuries. Carvery lunch, Sunday brunch, evening snacks. Pub grub. Tel: 478 4698.

Major Tom's, King St South. Music and memorabilia from the 60s & 70s. Open till 2 a.m. Pub grub. Tel: 478 3266.

The South William, William St South. Pub grub.

Break For The Border, Lower Stephen St, beside Grafton Plaza Hotel. Live music in Wild West style Wed-Sat. Restaurant, late bar, dancing till 2.30 a.m. Tel: 478 0300.

Gleesons, 18 Aungier St. Pub grub. Tel: 475 3808.

J.J Smyth, Aungier St. Pub grub.

Aungier House, 43 Aungier St. Pub grub. Tel: 475 3181.

O'Connell Street to Abbey Theatre

Starting from the Parnell monument at the top end of O'Connell Street, through to the Abbey Theatre and Eden Quay.

Airways Bar, 9 Findlater Place. Pub grub. Tel: 874 8491.

The Parnell, Parnell St. Excellent Irish stew.

Patrick Conway's, Moore Lane. Pub grub.

The Goalpost, 9 Cathedral St. Weekend music. Carvery & home-made dishes. Tel: 874 4868.

Barry Fitzgerald's, 90 Marlboro St. Pub grub. Tel: 874 4082.

Sean O'Casey's, 105 Marlborough St. Pub grub. Tel: 874 8675.

Flowing Tide, 9 Abbey St Lower. Handy for before or after theatre at the Abbey. Theatre posters cover walls and ceiling. Live music weekly. Pub grub. Tel: 874 0842.

The Plough, 28 Abbey St Lower. Very popular with Abbey theatre-goers, just across the road. Pub grub. Tel: 874 0971.

Lanigan's, Clifton Court Hotel, 11 Eden Quay. Live Irish music nightly and on weekend afternoons. Established 1822 with turf fires, beamed ceilings and candlelight. Traditional Irish food served all day. Tel: 874 3535.

The Liffey Inn, 28 Eden Quay. Tel: 874 5209.

Mary Street area

Slattery's, 129 Capel St. A highly rated pub for traditional music and blues. Paul Brady was a regular folk performer here in the 60s. Pub grub.

John M. Keating, 14 Mary St. Traditional session six nights a week. Full menu available. Pub grub. Tel: 873 1567.

The Coopers, 38 Abbey St Upper. Pub grub. Tel: 873 2946.

Off-centre locations

William Searson's, Upper Baggot St. Traditional Irish music and dancing. Carvery lunch, evening menu till 8 p.m.

The Brazen Head, 20 Lower Bridge St. Dates from 1666 on site of the original inn of 1198. Traditional music nightly. Tel: 679 5156.

11.4 Late night venues

Lower Leeson Street runs down from the south-eastern corner of St Stephen's Green, and is a popular night club and restaurant area. It doesn't really come to life until after midnight, when the pubs have closed.

Between midnight and 4 a.m., the area is generally known to Dubliners as The Stretch. When visiting these establishments, a well-padded credit card will be useful.

The scene changes with some rapidity. Check the listings magazines to find which clubs are currently 'in'.

Chapter Twelve

Go shopping

12.1 Shops and street markets

Shop hours are 9 to 17.30 or 18 hrs Mon-Sat; until 20 hrs on Thu.

For the best range of shops, stay around the Grafton Street area. For more down-to-earth prices, go to O'Connell Street and Henry Street – try Clerys department store, or Arnotts. If you're hunting for a particular book, start with Easons near the GPO.

High quality craft products, with prices to match, are available in the speciality shops of Nassau Street, such as Blarney Woollen Mills and The Kilkenny Shop for handloomed sweaters, Irish linen, Waterford Crystal, pottery etc; Kevin & Howlin for men's tweeds, hats and caps. The House of Ireland features traditional Irish gifts.

Dublin's largest shopping mall is St Stephen's Green, which promises "the ultimate shopping experience." It is a light and airy shopping centre in the modern idion with a glass atrium and lots of creamy-white paint everywhere.

This guidebook's personal vote goes to the Powerscourt Townhouse Centre (*see description in Chapter 5*). It offers a full range of boutiques, antique stores and one of Ireland's leading galleries. On the top floor is the Crafts Council Gallery, which displays high-grade ceramics, wooden items, furniture, handwoven items, metalcraft and basketware. Many of the craft products are like works of art.

Trendy browsing

Another trendy shopping district is Temple Bar, where browsing is delightful and where experimental and imaginative designers are finding their feet.

At weekends, along the park railings in Merrion Square, opposite the National Gallery, artists of varying talent display works for sale.

12.2 VAT rebates

Visitors from countries outside the European Union can reclaim the luxury Value Added Tax of 21% which is imposed on textiles, glass and similar products. The scheme operates from most high-grade stores which display a Cashback sticker. Check the details when making the purchase, and ask for a Cashback Voucher that is needed for claiming a refund.

With stamped vouchers of less than IR£200, instant repayments are given at the Cashback desk at Dublin Airport. For higher amounts, first have the receipts checked at the Customs booth in the Arrivals Hall. Leave enough spare time before check-in!

There is no refund on services, which are normally charged at 12.5%.

Chapter Thirteen

At your service

13.1 Changing money

Banks are open 10-16 hrs Monday to Friday (until 19 hrs on Thursday), but weekend visitors need not despair. Numerous exchange bureaux are open with more extended hours, particularly at the airport and at the Central Bus Station.

A commission rate of 1% is normal, but the airport exchange bureau makes a minimum commission charge of £2.50. The exchange bureau at the Dublin Tourism Centre is operated by American Express, and all major traveller cheques are exchanged free of commission. For cash the commission is 1%, with £1 minimum.

The exact exchange rate between the British pound and the Irish punt – written as IR£ – is roughly one to one. Sometimes the pound trails slightly behind. That means, if you change a hundred British pounds, you'll probably get ninety-something Irish pounds in exchange.

Many shops and cab-drivers will cheerfully accept English banknotes, subject to a small adjustment for the exchange difference. Likewise, credit card payments will reflect the current exchange rate when your monthly statement arrives.

To report a lost or stolen credit card – Access, Visa or Mastercard – contact freephone 1850 706 706.

Irish time and Electricity
The same as Britain.

The weather

Even the Irish talent for fantasy cannot convince you that the Republic is a land of blue skies. Come prepared for dampness in the air, to this country where there's no such thing as drought. On average Dublin has rain 12 days a month, but only 10 in February. Most people understand why the national colour is green.

Newspapers

Newspapers from UK are marked up in price, but are still less expensive than the local morning papers – *Irish Times* and *Irish Independent* – which retail at 85p. For comparison, when the cover price of the London *Times* is 30p, it sells in Dublin at 45p.

Telephone and Post

Most hotels operate an automated telephone system, which clocks up your usage automatically. But they will probably still make a service charge on top of their usual mark-up.

Local calls from a public phone box cost 20p. Phone cards are handier for long-distance and international calls. They are available from Post Offices and newsagents, and cost IR£2 for a 10-unit card, up to £16 for 100 units. International rates are cheaper at weekends, and on weekdays from 18 hrs until 8 o'clock next morning (or until midday to USA and Canada).

The Dublin area code is 01. To call Dublin from Britain, dial 00-353-1 + the local number. To call a UK number from Dublin, dial 00-44 + the area code without the initial zero + the local number.

For operator assistance to Britain, dial 10; for other international, dial 114.

Letter post to Britain and other EU countries is 32p, postcards 28p. Airmail to USA and other long-haul destinations is 52p for up to 20 grammes.

Main post offices offer fax services.

Public holidays
January 1; March 17 St Patrick's Day; Good Friday and Easter Monday; May 1; first Mondays in June and August, and the last Monday in October; December 25 and 26.

Consulates
American – Elgin Road, Ballsbridge, Dublin 4. Tel: 668 7122.
Australian – Fitzwilton House, Wilton Tec, Dublin 2. Tel: 676 1517.
British – 33 Merrion Road, Dublin 4. Tel 269 5211.
Canadian – 65-68 St Stephen's Green, Dublin 2. Tel: 478 1988.

More information
Irish Tourist Board
UK – 150 New Bond Street, London W1Y 0AQ. Tel: 0171-493 3201. Fax: 0171-493 9065.
USA – 345 Park Avenue, New York NY 10154. Tel: 418 0800.
Australia – 5th Level, 36 Carrington Street, Sydney 2000. Tel: 299 6177.
Canada – 160 Bloor East, Suite 1150, Toronto M1W 1B9. Tel: (416) 929 2777.

Dublin Tourism Centre, Suffolk Street, Dublin 2. Tel: accessible only from abroad (353)-1-605 7797; Fax: 605 7787. Information lines available only from within Eire, costing 58p per minute – Tel: 1550 112233; Fax: 1550 114400. Accommodation and ticket reservations by phone and credit card, with service charge: (353)-1-605 7777.

Dublin Event Guide – available on the Internet at http://www.events.homenet.ie/ for updated event listings.

Emergencies – Police, Fire, Ambulance dial 999.